POWER SHIFTS

*Five Forgotten Strategies
For Expanding God's Kingdom*

Dr. Howard Foltz

EQUIP PRESS

Colorado Springs

POWER SHIFTS

Published by Equip Press, Colorado Springs, CO

First Edition: 2019
Power Shifts / Dr. Howard Foltz
Paperback ISBN: 978-1-946453-69-3
eBook ISBN: 978-1-946453-70-9

EQUIP PRESS

Colorado Springs

CONTENTS

FOREWORD

Howard Foltz is a man with a mission. His is a commitment to God and to the task of world evangelization that puts most of us to shame. And this is a book to help us deal with that shame—if we hear and heed Foltz's call to practice mission according to several forgotten perspectives.

"It's clear that our times demand that we make an accounting for the missions 'status quo,' which has left half the world's population to die without ever hearing the Gospel." This is Foltz's assessment of the present situation in Christian missions. But we, like Esther, are here "for such a time as this." To Foltz, the situation is not hopeless. But we must change our perspective and our approach.

We don't know why God involves and even depends on us in His great program to win the world. It seems He has put certain limitations on Himself regarding His workings among humans. For, though He is not willing that any should perish (2 Peter 3:9), we are told that over 17 million people die without Christ every year. We may ask is this because God has not done His job?. Or is it because He has entrusted part of the job to us and we have not held up our end of the deal?

Stating that we need to plead guilty for not carrying out the mandate God has given us to communicate the gospel to all peoples everywhere (Mark 16:15), Dr. Foltz advocates a series of "power shifts" to enable us to function more effectively as God intended in world evangelization. Such power shifts would enable God's people "to utilize [their] spiritual resources in a higher level of productivity." The three conditions leading to this "higher level of productivity" are "prophetic vision, biblical wisdom, and comprehensive understanding and insight."

The book then goes on to discuss the application of this perspective in five basic areas. First, we need a change in attitude—from personal power to servanthood. Then we need to move from inaction, reaction, or destructive action to mobilized, constructive action. We will be known by what we do, not simply by what we think and say. Third, we must align ourselves with what God is doing rather than focusing, as we often do, on our plans and our structures. Our plans may often be pictured as machines, but God's analogies are usually agricultural. He plants seeds that grow and take their nourishment from whatever soil they land in. He does not build a machine that requires foreign expertise to fix when it breaks down.

The fourth power shift is to be in our recognition and utilization of resources. Foltz points out that among the peoples to whom we go, there is already an abundance of resources for support, growth, and all the rest waiting to be claimed for the Kingdom. We and they are flowing in a river of God's grace and blessings. We are to work with God in that abundance. The fifth shift, then, is in the area of anointing. We need to move from secular models of mission to seeing and dealing with the spiritual realities underlying both the opposition of receiving peoples and the lethargy of sending churches. God calls us to demonstrate His presence and love by countering satanic power with His power.

In this short book, Dr. Foltz alerts us to what he sees as the crucial shift needed to get the job of mission done—the power shift. He makes his points clearly, illustrates them well, and challenges us with a fresh vision of what to do and how to do it. May the reader hear and heed what he says. And may God bless you with the willingness to practice what Dr. Foltz preaches.

Rev. Dr. Charles H. Kraft
South Pasadena, CA

ACKNOWLEDGMENTS

The process of writing a book - especially a strategic book based on Scripture and intending to accelerate the rate at which the Church is building God's Kingdom - is never really the result of labor from just one person. It requires the incentive and inspiration offered by our Lord. But it also rests squarely on the shoulders of a supportive spouse as well as administrative assistants, editors, editorial assistants, proofreaders, and even my missions students at Regent University and partner churches with *Acceleration in Mission Strategies* (AIMS).

My wife, Pat, deserves more credit than words can express for her partnership in missionary ministry that began in 1963, one year into our marriage. During our Teen Challenge ministry in Texas and Eurasia, she prayed with drug addicts, hosted countless national leaders and even Regent University students in our home, administered our office, and became an "expert mover" as she packed and unpacked our belongings to move nine times. No one could have a better wife and partner in ministry than I do.

I also want to note the contribution of Rev. Dr. Charles H. Kraft, whose comments encouraged me, and who graciously agreed to write the foreword to this book. And, of course, I want to recognize the environment provided by AIMS, which offered the practical context within which I could reflect and write. I'm forever thankful for the dedication and creativity of the AIMS staff. Regent University furnished much of the academic context that supports this book.

I have also relied on countless authors, pastors, and other experts who loaned their expertise to me through their books, magazines, newsletters, and interviews. I am so grateful to all who prayed for and assisted in the development and production of this book.

ENDORSEMENTS

These seven thought-provoking chapters challenge us to reflect biblically, prophetically, and practically on our cherished mission worldview. Besides touching on practical strategies, this book gives a thorough, honest, biblical, and theological analysis of the subject.

Reverend Dr. Joshua Yee
Senior Pastor
Renewal Lutheran Church, Malaysia

Dr. Foltz has written a deeply probing, challenging book that dares us to face the realities of world missions. His book cuts like a finely honed double-edge sword. On the one side is a heart of compassion for the lost, and limitless energy toward the closure of the Great Commission. On the other side is a keen analytical mind uncovering divine laws he calls "power shifts" that, if obeyed, guarantee fulfillment of Jesus' command.

John Gilman
Founder / President
Dayspring International, Virginia Beach, VA

I have known Dr. Howard Foltz for over twenty years; first as a professor at Regent University and then as a missions mobilizer with AIMS. *Power Shifts: Five Forgotten Strategies for Expanding God's Kingdom* will challenge you to leave the status quo and find the new power shifts that are already happening in the mission field. We are entering the greatest harvest the Church has ever seen, and may we all have eyes to see the harvest before us.

Gordon Robertson,

CEO, The Christian Broadcasting Network

Dr. Foltz never fails to inspire and provoke me to think more strategically. He recoils against a "mission status quo" in order to tirelessly fight for the unsaved who haven't heard. As you ponder the principles on these pages, I pray they will inspire and challenge you to see the unreached, the Church, and yourself like you never have before!

Matt Beemer

Founder & International Director

Club 1040

Dr. Howard Foltz has written a powerful and desperately needed book for the entire Body of Christ. *Power Shifts* is straight from the heart of God and a message that every single believer should read. Following the precepts in this book will take us from the Great Commission to the Great Completion.

Dr. Foltz brilliantly points out that we need far more than a paradigm shift within Christianity regarding the Great Commission. We must have five very strategic power shifts.

Read with expectation and anticipation of God doing GREAT things in your life, He is waiting on you to respond.

Pastor Mark Cowart

Senior Pastor

Church For All Nations, Colorado Springs, CO

"Your heart for mission inspired me in a big way! Thanks for sowing a seed in my life."

Mark Batterson

New York Times best-selling author of *The Circle Maker*

Lead Pastor of National Community Church

1

HOW CAN WE MULTIPLY THE HARVEST?

Please think deeply about the following statistics. Each year, about 60 million people die worldwide. Of these, about 17 million will go into eternity without hearing about a Heavenly Father who loves them and sent His Son to purchase their salvation! That's equal to 46,575 people per day, 1,940 per hour, 32 per minute, and about one every two seconds![1]

> Each year, about 60 million people die worldwide; about 17 million will go into eternity without hearing about a Heavenly Father. That's equal to 46,575 people per day, 1,940 per hour, 32 per minute, and about one every two seconds!

For most of us, these are shocking statistics. For me, they scream "Emergency!" This is the worst human crisis on earth. Many of these people have never "rubbed shoulders" with a Catholic, Orthodox, or Evangelical Christian. Yet the very last words of Jesus were,

But you will receive power when the Holy Spirit comes on you;
and you will be my witnesses in Jerusalem, and in all Judea and
Samaria, and to the ends of the earth. (Acts 1:8)

Obviously, contemporary ministry must change, and we need a new army of missionaries that will cross the dark chasm of culture, political, and language barriers to reach "the ends of the earth," that is, the 3.14 billion people who live in 7,066 unreached people groups* around the world. The Great Commission of Jesus, in all the Gospels as well as Acts 1:8, and these contemporary statistics, represent the greatest humanitarian need and social justice issue confronting the church today.

Now, let's admit right up front that traditional missionary methods have enjoyed a certain level of success. After all, the first Christians were from the Jewish community. For them, accepting Jesus as their Messiah had absolutely nothing to do with cross-cultural outreach.

But if you are from a Gentile ethnic background, clearly you are a believer today because, somewhere along the way, someone stepped across cultural barriers to proclaim the Gospel where it had not yet been heard. You may be the product of a family that came to the Lord many, many generations ago. But your salvation is still the long-term result of some type of missionary outreach. In the 2,000 years since our Lord's ascension, when He gave the Great Commission to go into all the world and make disciples, His followers have successfully built His Kingdom in vast regions of this earth.

Yet, despite that success, we also have huge regions left almost entirely unevangelized. Only God knows the actual number of individuals who remain untouched by the gospel.

Accounting for the "Status Quo"

The world's current spiritual environment demands that we make an accounting for the missions "status quo." Despite our earnest efforts, statisticians say that over 41% of our global population of 7.6 billion people have yet to hear about God's gracious offer of salvation. That includes the people we mentioned before, who have the potential to die without ever meeting a Christian of any kind. It also includes those who live in cultures

---

* All unreached people statistics are from www.joshuaproject.net.

where the gospel has perhaps been presented, but not in a culturally relevant way that most people can understand.

During His ministry on earth, Jesus told His disciples,

The harvest is plentiful but the workers are few. Ask the Lord of the harvest, therefore, to send out workers into his harvest field. (Mt. 8:37–38)

Obviously, we need to pray for more laborers to accept the responsibility of taking the gospel to the ends of the earth.

And we need not pray gently. The word translated "send out" in the original language actually means "to eject, cast out, drive out, or expel."[2] That means we are to intercede on behalf of the nations, asking God to drive believers out of their comfort zones and into service and ministry to others.

But is that all God wants us to do? I think not. The Parable of the Sower, found in Matthew 13:1–23 and Mark 4:8, gives us intriguing hope for multiplied bounty in the spiritual harvest, 30, 60, and 100-fold.

Exponential Harvest

You may think that agrarian thinking is not relevant to you. After all most of us know little to nothing about "farming." However, living in an agrarian society, Jesus often used agricultural terms and stories to illustrate the principles of His Kingdom. These stories and principles still speak to us today. In the Parable of the Sower, Jesus compared the gospel to seeds scattered by a farmer. Some seed fell along a path, and birds descended and gobbled it up before it had an opportunity to sprout. Other seed fell on rocky places and sprang up quickly, but then it died because the stones hindered the growth of the supporting roots. Other seed fell among thorns, which grew up and choked out the young seedlings. But some seed fell on good soil. These seeds grew and produced a tremendous harvest.

The spiritual lesson of this parable seems to be fairly easy to interpret—the yield depends on the quality of the soil. That's what we've always heard, right? Yet, as I pondered this parable, I saw an important point that I had missed before. You see, the good soil was pretty much all the same. Jesus made no distinction in its quality or its preparation. Yet, even in the good soil, the harvest varied. Jesus said, "It produced a crop —a hundred, sixty or thirty times what was sown" (Mt. 13:8).

What made the difference? Why did some seed reproduce itself thirty times, while other seed exponentially multiplied that harvest, reproducing itself even one hundred times?

That question is the focus of this book. God alone makes this world's spiritual harvest fields ripen at the correct time. Yet He invites us to participate in the process of clearing away obstacles, sowing spiritual seed, and bringing in the crops. In that process, I believe we can hasten or slow the rate at which we are accomplishing the task our Lord gave us just before He returned to heaven—the task of taking the gospel of His Kingdom to every people group in the world.

Agricultural Lessons

In biblical days, people farmed by sheer muscle and willpower. They cleared fields, tilled soil, planted seed, harvested crops, and prepared grain— all by hand. In some regions of the world, people still farm that way. But in Western industrialized nations, modern machinery, fertilizers, hybrid seeds, and irrigation systems have dramatically increased the yield of grain on an acre of land.

In missions, we must willingly follow that example. We need to quit patting ourselves on the backs for our thirtyfold harvest and start looking for ways to harvest a hundredfold yield. **We must rethink some of our basic ideas about taking the gospel to the ends of the earth.** Just as farmers have increased their yield by accepting and using new implements and tools, we need to be willing to give up our teams of oxen, so to speak, in favor of tractors and combines. We need to examine and evaluate our methods and open our hearts to **new patterns of thinking.** I call these dramatic, foundational modifications "strategic power shifts."

More Than Toffler's Power Shifts

Many people are familiar with the book, *Power Shifts*, by Alvin Toffler.[3] It discusses power moving from here to there, or from this person to that person. In other words, Toffler says a power shift occurs when one group of people loses power and another group gains power, such as in a political uprising. Let me say up front that, while I refer to this definition because so many people are already familiar with it, <u>this is not how I define power shifts for the missions community.</u>

I don't believe we necessarily need a shift of power from one place to another or from one person to another. Rather, I believe we need to do the equivalent of hitting the "shift" key on a keyboard, or even a font change on a computer. We need to quit settling for "power" and move instead to "POWER." We need to leverage our resources to a new level and exponentially multiply the results we see on the mission field.

More Than a Paradigm Shift

I also need to note that my use of the term "power shift" is not the same as a "paradigm shift." Paradigm became a hot-button term in the 1990s. It was used so much that sometimes I wonder if we even really agree about what it means, so let's go ahead and define it.

> "Power shift" is not the same as a "paradigm shift." Paradigm relates to our worldview, and it is the sum of our "mental filters," through which we define reality.

Paradigm is a Greek word that, until recently, was used most frequently as a scientific term. In present-day usage, it means "a pattern, an outline, a theory, or a perception." More loosely, it is an assumption or a frame of reference. **Paradigm relates to our worldview, and it is the sum of our "mental filters," through which we define reality.**

A paradigm shift, then, is a change in our worldview, which, in turn, affects the way we interpret reality. Let's look at several examples.

In astronomy, Ptolemy pronounced the earth to be the center of the universe in 140 AD. His assertion affected the way people viewed reality.

Copernicus came along, and after much study, he concluded in 1543 AD that Ptolemy was wrong—the celestial bodies revolve around the sun. Copernicus, of course, was right, but his ideas were initially considered heretical because He placed the sun, not man, at the center of the universe. When acceptance came, this change in thinking generated a paradigm shift in people's "mental filters." Long term, this altered the course of physical science and theological understanding. Hence, a power shift resulted.

In another arena, ancient Greeks attested to the fact that the earth is round. But succeeding generations lost that idea, coming to believe that the world was flat. When opinion leaders eventually experienced a paradigm shift and came to accept that the world is round, they also unleashed a power shift because they initiated a new level of exploration, commerce, and colonization all over the world.

It's important to note from the preceding examples that paradigm shifts are not the same as power shifts; however, they generally do precede power shifts. It stands to reason, then, that if we truly want to experience an exponential release of God's power, we need to get a handle on His paradigm. "My thoughts are not your thoughts," God has reminded us, "neither are your ways my ways" (Is. 55:8). We must tune in to His thoughts and His ways if we are to accomplish anything that really matters for eternity.

More Than Revival

We can't determine God's thoughts and His overarching plan through revival alone. Even the great Reformation did little to build a missions emphasis or to release workers into the harvest field. Therefore, if the Church is ever going to bring closure or completion to the Great Commission that Christ laid before us almost 2,000 years ago—the task of taking the gospel throughout the world (Matt. 28:18-20; Acts 1:8)—then we must enlarge our vision to accept His thoughts on missions.

Since Christ gave the church this task, we must accept the fact that it can be done. This alone will be a huge paradigm shift for many Christians. However, since two thousand years of effort have not brought completion, we must face the need for a strategic power shift if, indeed, we intend to bring completion to the Great Commission.

But we must always understand that **we do not produce strategic power shifts by ourselves. The Holy Spirit births every strategic power shift. We produce them only as we engage ourselves with God and move in partnership with Him, accepting His strategic direction.** Then, out of our relationship with Him, we can multiply our spiritual harvest in an exponential manner. And it will be for His glory.

Strategic Missions Power Shifts

Now, let's determine what a strategic missions **power shift** is—for the purpose of this book, we're defining the term like this: **the employment of prophetic vision, biblical wisdom, and comprehensive understanding and insight to utilize spiritual resources in a higher level of productivity.** Let's take that definition apart.

> A power shift is: the employment of prophetic vision, biblical wisdom, and comprehensive understanding and insight to utilize spiritual resources in a higher level of productivity.

Vision: Seeing What God Sees

Most of us are familiar with Proverbs 29:18:

Where there is no revelation, the people cast off restraint; but blessed is he who keeps the law.

Literally, from many different sources, this is what the verse means: "Without a continuous redemptive revelation of God's will, the people of God are allowed to go without direction and are wasting away."[4]

The bottom line here is that, without a clear, ongoing understanding of God's redemptive nature—a vision of God and what He is doing in our world and in our covenant relationship with Him—we will lack direction. Without that continuous vision that helps us connect with what He sees and feels, we will waste away.

Have you ever been in a church that's wasting away? I have. I've been in some churches where you would need a jackhammer to cut through the wastedness. You could cut it and then stack it in the corner because it was so concrete. Recently, I heard of a church that has gone year after year without a single convert. The pastor was asked, "Can you believe God for one convert next year?" His comment, "I don't think so."

Do you know what's happened in churches like that? Generally, the leaders and the laity have gone so long without an up-to-date revelation of what God is doing in the world—what He is seeing and feeling and saying—that they've lost their vision or inspiration. They are somewhere in the process of wasting away from what God intends them to be. If we are to avoid being lost in that kind of wasteland, we must seek, through studying God's Word and through every other avenue open to us, to maintain a clear vision of His redemptive nature and a clear understanding of His priorities for ministry.

Wisdom from the Word and the Spirit

Studying the Bible to gain God's wisdom enables us to become what Scripture calls an "expert builder" or "master builder." Paul noted,

> *By the grace God has given me, I have laid a foundation as an expert builder, and someone else is building on it. But each one should be careful how he builds. (1 Cor. 3:10)*

The term "expert builder" in the original Greek is *sophos architekton*. You can see the logical connection with our word "architect." An "expert builder" is one who is competent in his profession and applies wisdom and skill to his task.[5]

Of course, in the spiritual realm, we replace human wisdom and skill with Scripture and with God's guidance. We get alone with the Lord. We stand before Him with His Word and ask Him to give strategic direction to help us build on the foundation of Jesus Christ and raise up spiritual generations. In this sense, the "expert builder" is like the Apostle Paul himself. He is a leader who sees what the Father is doing by the Word and by the Spirit, and he governs his life and makes decisions based on the knowledge and wisdom he gains from that relationship. This is a spiritual skill.

Comprehensive Insight

Biblical vision and wisdom enable us to see "the big picture" of God's will, thus giving birth to comprehensive understanding and insight. Colossians 1:9 records Paul's intercession on behalf of the church at Colossae, as he noted, "For this reason, since the day we heard about you, **we have not stopped praying for you and asking God to fill you with the knowledge of his will through all spiritual wisdom and understanding.**"

The word translated as "understanding" is the Greek word *sunesis*, **which means "putting pieces together like a puzzle." It is the critical factor that enables an individual to intelligently assess a situation.**[6]

In our contemporary world, we need to seek that kind of *sunesis*. We need to apply God's contemporary wisdom with an understanding of "the big picture." We need to see the forest and not just the trees. We need to move beyond our own little corner of the harvest field and gain an understanding of God's plan for the entire farm, or world.

This requires that we watch trends on a worldwide basis and seek God's wisdom for how we can exploit them for His glory. We must understand that He is orchestrating the world scene to accomplish His goals because He is heading for the completion of the Great Commission.

For instance, when China opened its doors for Westerners to come as English teachers, some trend-watching Christians saw it as a tremendous opportunity for evangelism. They mobilized, trained, and sent Christians to fill those positions. Because some brave believers took advantage of this opportunity, engaging in lifestyle and friendship evangelism, thousands of house churches exist in regions where the gospel had not been heard.

Sanctified trend watching, with a vision for evangelism and discipleship, is reaping tremendous harvest all over the world.

Increased Productivity from Spiritual Resources

Strategic power shifts should produce an exponential multiplication of the numbers of people finding Christ. The concepts defined in this power shift are not intended to be ends in themselves. They are means to discover new ways to use our spiritual resources to move from the thirtyfold harvest to the hundredfold harvest.

The caution here is that momentum, in my opinion, is a clear ingredient in the multiplication process. **Missing a strategic missions power shift can actually drop us to a lower level of inertia or even to regression. This type of power shift is a regressive slide.**

> Missing a strategic missions power shift can actually drop us to a lower level of inertia or even to regression. This type of power shift is a regressive slide.

In the physical world, we can learn a lesson from the arena of space travel. We've all watched TV broadcasts of rocket and shuttle launches. We've seen the brilliant flames erupt from underneath the spacecraft. We've watched those marvelous vehicles hesitate briefly and then break free from the confines of gravity as they soared toward lofty realms beyond our experience.

Did you know that the space shuttle will burn more fuel at lift-off than it will in traveling one million miles through space? That's because, as it accelerates away from the launch pad, it must overcome inertia and gravity.

The same is true in our spiritual lives. Remember, we said earlier that the literal translation of Proverbs 29:18 implies that we must have a continuous redemptive vision of God. That must be the source of our spiritual momentum, which enables us to avoid regressing and eventually wasting away.

For Such a Time as This

This phrase, of course, comes from the book of Esther, when her uncle Mordecai convinced her to act as a mediator on behalf of the Jewish people, who were facing annihilation at the hands of Haman. "Do not think that because you are in the king's house you alone of all the Jews will escape," he told his niece, who was the king's wife.

> *For if you remain silent at this time, relief and deliverance for the Jews will arise from another place, but you and your father's family will perish.* **And who knows but that you have come to royal position for such a time as this? (Esther 4:12-14)**

How about us? Are we not "God's chosen people, a royal priesthood" for such a time as this? (1 Pet. 2:9).

In other words, just like the Jewish population faced extermination in that day, so in our day, millions of individuals all over the world are spiritually perishing. How many of us have the same feelings that Mordecai cautioned Esther against? Perhaps we wrongly feel safe because we live in the comparative physical and spiritual wealth of the Western world. In a similar situation, Mordecai reminded Queen Esther that security does not automatically come because of where we live.

Security, however, is found in obedience to the revealed Word of God. If we refuse to obey, God will raise up another who will do as He requires. All tribes and nations will be represented in heaven, for God has promised it in Matthew 24:14.

> *And this gospel of the kingdom will be preached in the whole world as a testimony to all nations (Gr. Ethne or people groups), and then the end will come.*

Yet our refusal to obey may certainly impact the eternal destiny of specific individuals within those people groups. And we will have missed the opportunity and the honor of partnering with Him in an activity or event that takes on miraculous proportions. And in the end, we will also miss the blessing of fellowship with Him as we labor in partnership to fulfill His greatest desire—bringing people into His Kingdom from every people group in the world.

The remainder of this book will outline five overarching strategic power shifts, which I believe will help provide the fuel to launch local churches, mission agencies, and individuals into understanding and accomplishing God's will to fulfill the Great Commission.

I pray that you will read with an open mind and that you will seek God's wisdom regarding these five issues. As they ignite spiritual rockets in you, put these theories into practice. I pray that you will find God as your partner, enabling you to discover a whole new level of productivity that perhaps you had never dreamed possible. And as you continuously renew your redemptive vision of God through the things you see Him doing around the world, may you know His fellowship in a greater way as you seek to know His thoughts and His ways.

A Glimpse of a Strategic Power Shift in Action

In this chapter, we saw the graphic need to "power shift" from status quo missions to strategic, multiplying missions. Actually, it's an "Emergency!" Just think, 41.4% of the people on planet earth are unreached. They live in people groups where they have no access to the gospel—no missionary, no church, no Bible—shut out from hearing about God's love for them. We need to answer this bleak, Satan-controlled situation with a fresh "strategic power shift" that will move the church toward obeying and completing the Great Commission.

I work with a dedicated team of highly committed people in a ministry called Acceleration In Mission Strategies or AIMS. Our mission is to be "Your Partner in Strategic Missions." God has given us a vision and some biblical wisdom that leads to "how to put the evangelism and discipling puzzle together" to reach unreached people groups. As a team, we fully honor the grace of God that has given us a methodology by which we aim to be a part of completing the Great Commission.

AIMS' has an initiative called LIGHT 3500. BHAG is a famous acronym that stands for Big Hairy Audacious Goal. Our LIGHT 3500 BHAG (Big *Holy* Audacious Goal) is to see a team of individuals, churches, and organizations "adopt" 3,500 unreached people groups, totaling 2.5 billion lost souls. These are called "Frontier People Groups" because less than 0.01% are born again, some even 0.0% born again! You and I wouldn't want to live where they live. These are the darkest places on earth:

We look for light, but all is darkness; for brightness, but we walk in deep shadows. Like the blind we grope along the wall, feeling our way like people without eyes. At midday we stumble as if it were twilight; among the strong, we are like the dead. (Isa. 59:9–10)

To "adopt" means to adopt in prayer and action to see these 3,500 people groups have the light of the gospel. This means that a "born again" movement in their midst will move them to at least 2% evangelical. Churches (even underground) will be planted and the Kingdom of God will break through in their culture.

> To "adopt" means to adopt in prayer and action to see these 3,500 people groups have the light of the gospel.

LIGHT 3500 has several layers of internet training for its partners. This means that partners from any online country in the world can be trained and know how to work together. We also have trained online coaches to guide partners in this strategy.

To learn more about LIGHT 3500 and how you can become involved in this "strategic power shift," visit www.aims.org. Let's believe God for millions of souls to come out of darkness into the light of His Kingdom.

Pause, Reflect, Pray, Plan

1. Does your personal ministry need "power shifts"? Be open, honest, even vulnerable.

2. List the two or three that are most important.

_____

_____

_____

_____

3. Ask God for a plan to leverage each of these into a positive power shift.

_____

_____

_____

_____

2

POWER SHIFT #1—ATTITUDE

L ife is like a game of tennis," a wise person once said. "The player who serves well seldom loses."[1]

We smile at this phrase, perhaps even recognize its truth, but few of us are eager to live a life characterized by service. *The Ugly American*, a 1958 novel describing the authors' opinion that much of American diplomacy in Asia was folly, gives secular examples of those who refused to serve and also those who made a tremendous difference because they chose to serve. At certain points, the authors speak through Asian journalists. One named U Maung Swe tells an American ambassador, "A mysterious change seems to come over Americans when they go to a foreign land. They isolate themselves socially. They live pretentiously. They're loud and ostentatious."[2]

Another young journalist named Ruth Jyoti visited the U.S. and was asked to speak at a dinner meeting for the San Francisco press.

> *"Generally," she said, "Americans in Asia are not effective. They are what I call the Intellectual Maginot Line. They feel that if the nice, rich, respectable people like them, they must be doing a good job. I can understand that. You look at foreign faces, hear strange languages—and you just feel more comfortable at the Press Club or*

the American Club or the Officer's Club. Or anywhere where quiet
people are wearing collars and ties."³

Yet, she says, a few Americans are effective in her region. One person in particular, a man named Bob Maile, "did more to raise American prestige than anyone else over there." How did he do it? "Instead of barging in at the top with the air of an ambassador, Bob Maile started off by trying to become familiar with our language and country." He made friends with the common people—the laborers. "He did these things without asking for credit or telling anyone. In return, he wanted tutoring in our language, lessons in our cooking and help in getting his children into our schools. He was humble about everything, and he made it clear that he thought he was getting more than he was giving."⁴

That, in a nutshell, is a true example of service. If the secular world can learn this lesson, surely we who claim to follow Christ can do at least as well as they. Roy Hession, in his Christian classic *The Calvary Road*, notes,

Nothing is clearer from the New Testament than that the Lord Jesus expects us to take the low position of servants. This is not just an extra obligation which we may or may not assume as we please. It is the very heart of that new relationship which the disciple is to take up with respect to God and his fellows if he is to know fellowship with Christ and any degree of holiness in his life.⁵

Yet the God Who requires this from us does not expect us to accomplish it on our own. We have His empowering Spirit, and we also have our Lord's words and example. "The greatest among you will be your servant," He said (Mt. 23:11), but He also demonstrated His commitment to service through His lifestyle, enabling Paul to later write,

Your attitude should be the same as that of Christ Jesus: Who, being in very nature God, did not consider equality with God something to be grasped, but made himself nothing, *taking the very nature of a servant*." (Phil. 2:5-7, italics added)

In our contemporary missions environment, our ability to make a lasting change in this world depends largely on our ATTITUDE. We are compelled to develop or renew a commitment to servanthood, based on the words and example of Christ. We must move from an attitude of only POWER and POSITION to one of SERVICE.

Strength in Servanthood

John 13:1-17 records Jesus' actions in the upper room at the Passover Feast just before His ordeal of suffering and death. The writer does not present Christ as a weak individual, resigned to a terrible fate He knew was on the horizon. Rather, he shows Jesus as an incredibly strong individual who chose to serve rather than demand.

> *"Jesus knew that the Father had put all things under his power,"* *John noted, "and that he had come from God and was returning to God; so he got up from the meal, took off his outer clothing, and wrapped a towel around his waist. After that, he poured water into a basin and began to wash his disciples' feet, drying them with the towel that was wrapped around him" (John 13:3-5).*

Now, I don't mean to become grammatical, but there is a great truth here. That little word "so" is like a hinge on which the rest of this passage hangs. It's the conjunction that holds everything together and demonstrates the relationship of the clauses to one another. It implies that Jesus' understanding of His power undergirded His desire and ability to serve. In short, this passage says, "Jesus knew... and <u>so</u> He washed...."

The Greek tense used here—imperfect present active—also indicates that, without the resultant action of serving, the power of the verb in that initial phrase would be nullified. That means the resultant action makes everything else that Jesus teaches come alive and exist in reality. The implication, of course, is that Jesus knew His authority—the Greek word is *exousia*, which means "delegated authority."[6]—had one purpose, and that was to do His Father's will. A revelation of the meaning of His *exousia* led Him to lay it down to serve—not pick it up in a display of majesty.

Authority with Purpose

After He washed His disciples' feet, Jesus asked them, "Do you understand what I have done for you? ...Now that I, your Lord and Teacher, have washed your feet, you also should wash one another's feet. I have set you an example that you should do as I have done for you... Now that you know these things, you will be blessed if you do them. (John 13:12–17)

Jesus challenges His followers to cultivate the same attitude that He had. He set us an example. We must choose to serve those who are lost and to disciple and nurture those in the Church. The result of that kind of attitude adjustment will unleash a power shift as we come to understand God's design for how His power is to be used. John 17 records Jesus' prayer just before His arrest.

"Father, the time has come," He said. "Glorify your Son, that your Son may glorify you. For you granted him authority over all people that he might give eternal life to all those you have given him" (verses 1–2).

The authority and power God gives for the purpose of bringing salvation to all people is also revealed in Matthew 28:18–20, "Then Jesus came to them and said,

All authority in heaven and on earth has been given to me. Therefore, *go and make disciples of all nations, baptizing them in the name of the Father and of the Son and of the Holy Spirit, and teaching them to obey everything I have commanded you. And surely I am with you always, to the very end of the age.*

We have another hinge here—the word "therefore." It shows the relationship between the two parts of this passage. Authority and power are given for a specific purpose. We are to use our "delegated authority" to make disciples of all nations, even those at the "ends of the earth." Also, it is important to know that as "Go and Preach" in Mark 16:15 is an imperative Greek word, so is "make disciples" here in Matthew 28:19. Go, preach, and make disciples are the foundational servant actions in building God's Kingdom, and they represented power shifts for the apostles.

Three Kinds of Servant

New Testament Greek presents an additional challenge to service, which is not immediately evident in translation. The original language of Greek uses at least three different applicable words for *servant*, each of which has its own connotation.[7]

> **Three Kinds of Servants**
> 1. Doulos
> 2. Diakanos
> 3. Huperetes

Doulos

This individual is a slave who is bound to his master so closely that only death can break the yoke. Romans 6 uses this term to offer a metaphor for our enslavement to sin. The picture here comes from the culture of the day in which it was written, when a convicted murderer would be bound to his dead victim and sentenced to carry around the body. The resulting decay eventually would kill the murderer as well. Paul challenged us to die to sin, for that is the only release, and to be bound instead to Christ.

Don't you know that when you offer yourselves to someone to obey him as slaves, you are slaves to the one whom you obey—whether you are slaves to sin, which leads to death, or to obedience, which leads to righteousness? But thanks be to God that, though you used to be slaves to sin, you wholeheartedly obeyed the form of teaching to which you were entrusted. You have been set free from sin and **have become slaves to righteousness.** *(Rom. 6:16–18)*

Diakanos

This word has come to be *deacon* in English. This individual attends to the needs of another. While *doulos* generally refers to a servant in relationship to his master, *diakonos* stresses the servant's relationship to his work.

> *Jesus called them together and said, "You know that the rulers of the Gentiles lord it over them, and their high officials exercise authority over them. Not so with you. Instead, whoever wants to become great among you must be your <u>servant (diakonos)</u>, and whoever wants to be first must be your <u>slave</u> (doulos)— just as the Son of Man did not come to be served, but to serve, and to give his life as a ransom for many." (Matt. 20:25-28)*

Huperetes

This word literally translated is "under-oarsmen." In Roman sailing vessels, there were helmsmen and rowers. The *huperetes* were the ones who performed the hardest work, for every time they drew their oars, they put them into the very teeth of the waves. Acts 13:36 uses this term when it notes, **"By the will of God, David <u>served</u> his generation..." The picture here is that, because he understood God's will, the king of all Israel humbled himself and chose to become an under-oarsman, taking on the hardest and least honored role he could imagine.**

Living Servanthood

Jesus was a *servant* in all three ways. He showed Himself as a *doulos* when He bound Himself to us, taking on human form and experiencing the pain and disappointment of life on earth, dying our death, and rising again for our salvation and God's glory. He revealed Himself as a *diakonos* when He fed people and when He ministered healing. And, though Paul chose to use a different word, Jesus demonstrated the characteristics of a *huperetes* when He "humbled himself and became obedient to death—even death on a cross" (Phil. 2:8).

Servanthood in Missions

Pius Wakatama was born in Africa and became a Christian at a mission station. He was educated in mission schools and then in the U.S., after which he returned home to teach at the college level in Africa. Writing in the 1970s, Wakatama stated this opinion:

> *I believe that the attitudinal qualifications of today's missionary must be summed up in the word servant [italics added]. They must take the principles of mission from the Great Missionary himself. He was a humble and lowly servant who took time to listen, to share and even to receive from those he came to minister to. He helped people without demeaning them, but preserved their dignity and human pride.*[8]

Though he wrote that statement many years ago, it is still true. Within the missions community and Christian ministry as a whole, the shift in *attitude* from personal power and position to servanthood has the potential to rock the status quo. None of us can create an exhaustive list of God's strategies for change—we can never measure or contain His creativity. Still, I have thought long and hard about how God wants the contemporary mission community—the people, organizations, and churches He has raised up for this time—to apply the principle of servanthood. He has given the overall picture, and now I believe He also wants to give us a specific plan that will enable us to multiply the power available for an explosive harvest. He has laid on my heart four applications that are particularly appropriate for the age in which we live.

1. Recognize the Best in All Cultures

We must move from an attitude of cultural imperialism to one of recognizing the best in all cultures. The novel referenced earlier in this chapter, *The Ugly American*, is full of examples of cultural imperialism, from an ambassador and staff who refuse to learn the local language, to a host of American diplomats who refuse to socialize with anyone outside the confines of their own compounds. In a factual epilogue, the authors explain, "The kind of ingrown social life portrayed in the story... is real.... The Asians themselves have given it a name." That name is "S.I.G.G." which stands for "Social Incest in the Golden Ghetto."[9]

Unfortunately, the Christian missionary community has not been completely immune to these same attitudes. Certainly, many Christian missionaries have made every effort to become servants in their adopted cultures. Pius Wakatama lists several things that traditional missionaries did right.

> *"Despite the negative side of missionary involvement in colonization,"* *he writes, "we should thank God that missionaries were involved.* *They helped in tempering the cruel excesses of their countrymen,* *and in many cases pleaded successfully for the rights of indigenous* *populations. Some of them stood up for nationals at great costs."*

He also points out that missionaries provided education, often in opposition to their home governments who wanted to keep a handle on their "cheap labor." And, he adds, many indigenous populations found personal freedom and self-worth from reading Scripture, often lovingly translated into an indigenous language by missionaries who began with a language that was limited to oral expression, and who laboriously created dictionaries and grammars before they were even able to begin the actual task of translation.

However, it is also true that mistakes were made, sometimes because of arrogance, and sometimes simply because of a lack of training or because of misinformation received during training. As Wakatama explains, "Because of ignorance as well as ethnic pride, missionaries have often exhibited a negative attitude toward other cultures. They have looked on them as aberrations, their own being the norm. In some cases, they have followed the example of the Judaizers in the early church, insisting that other people take on their cultural ways upon being Christians." Wakatama cites several examples, including clothing, social ceremonies, dancing, and music forms, etc. He later adds, "I am afraid some in the West mistake technological superiority for overall cultural superiority and have thus failed to appreciate and even benefit from other cultures."[10]

As a missionary, I've lived in several different cultures, and I've visited many more. All of them have positive and negative points. Those of us who live and work in the missions community might think we've moved well beyond this level of elitism, but we need to re-examine our motives and our strategies to make sure we aren't harboring any vestiges of superior feelings. We must not pass on Western culture as if it were the gospel. Our goal is to make disciples—not to make carbon copy Americans, or Asians, or Africans. That type of cultural ego limits our ability to adapt and bond with nationals, and that, in turn, limits our ability to serve in a cross-cultural context.

But even beyond that, cultural imperialism also squashes our understanding of the need to prepare adequately for ministering in a new society. I'm amazed at the people who come to me and say, "I've been a pastor," or "I have a degree in business, or communications, or whatever... I'm going to the mission field." They think being a missionary is a snap. They don't think they need to study cross-cultural communication or anthropology or missions strategy. They don't think they need to study anything. They just want to go to the mission field and "do it." Too often, they mess it up royally. And sometimes the devil takes them by the throat and squashes all the spiritual vigor from their ministry, and they go home personally defeated and a missionary failure.

Perhaps this is why one missions agency president wrote,

I believe it's common knowledge that most American Christians—even those in churches that are strong on missions—hold a stereotype of the typical missionary as a well-intentioned but somewhat naive person of limited ability who probably could not hold down a good job in the home country. The stereotype is unfair, but there are enough missionaries like that to reinforce the image of mediocrity.[11]

Being trained appropriately as a missionary is as important as being trained appropriately as a doctor. After all, ministering to a person's spiritual health is at least as important as ministering to his physical health. Pius Wakatama believes missionaries should meet qualifications in three specific areas: spiritual, academic, and attitude. Within his discussion on academic qualifications, he writes,

> *Many Christian colleges have become sensitive to the need for cross-cultural understanding in the field of communications, social psychology, anthropology of religions and many others.... Missionaries thus trained are able to witness more effectively to people of other cultures. They are also better able to assist them in thinking out their faith in reference to their cultural environments, thus formulating theologies which are expressed in indigenous thought forms and familiar terminology.*[12]

2. Indigenization

> I've talked to many Africans who have told me, "I'm a national leader, and we have many missionaries in our country, but I've never once sat in the front room or the kitchen of a missionary's home."

We must move from entrenchment to an attitude of indigenization. Wakatama's quote leads right into this point. You see, we have a history of developing a "missions compound mentality." **I've talked to many Africans who have told me, "I'm a national leader, and we have many missionaries in our country, but I've never once sat in the front room or the kitchen of a missionary's home."** I call that entrenchment—entrenching into our own culture and not opening ourselves up in vulnerability to our national brothers and sisters and the emerging leaders. The result is a retrenchment into a control-oriented leadership style, thus failing to indigenize the ministry. This also teaches nationals control-oriented leadership rather than modeling servant-oriented leadership.

The Ugly American includes a report from a fictional Soviet ambassador. He writes home to Moscow,

> *The American Ambassador is a jewel. He keeps his people tied up with meetings, social events, and greeting and briefing the scores of senators, congressmen, generals, admirals, undersecretaries of State and Defense, and so on, who come pouring through here to 'look for themselves.' He forbids his people to 'go into the hills,' and still annoys the people... with his bad manners.*[13]

Unfortunately, many Western missionaries have been guilty of portraying this same attitude. It's easy for Americans to be with Americans and Asians to be with Asians, etc. In that environment, we tend to withdraw from the very people we're called to serve. As quickly as possible, we need to indigenize the churches we are planting and the ministries we are initiating in cross-cultural situations. This means we must respect and empower national leaders with the authority necessary to build the church or the ministry that will exponentially multiply the harvest in their own culture and in others as well.

Stephen E. Saint is the son of Nate Saint, who was among the missionaries murdered in 1956 by the Auca Indians. Steve returned to the Huaorani (Aucas) in 1995 at their invitation to live and work among them. Later he wrote,

> **The harsh reality I encountered as I returned was that the Huaorani church of the mid-nineties was less functional than it had been in the early sixties."** *The root of the problem, I eventually realized, was that insidious disease that has sucked the life out of many Native American tribes and continues to devastate many ethnic communities within North and South America today—dependency. The Huaorani have become dependent on outsiders—especially North American Christians—for education, for medical and dental services, and for radio communications to relay information between their many villages.*

Saint admits that some of the problems have been created by "oil companies, government agencies, and other special interest groups that stand to benefit directly from that dependency," but that should not be true of Christ's Church. As Saint explains,

Unlike oil companies, the church has a lot to lose from creating dependency. **While most missionaries would not consciously foster dependency, I believe the Devil deceives us into creating this state by prompting us to mix into our legitimate desire to help others with a small measure of pride and a dose of cultural arrogance.**[14]

These attitudes are insidious, and they can creep into the most well-meaning of strategies. In the world of missions, we must take every precaution against this kind of superior attitude. We must encourage and enable indigenous congregations to be truly strong in the Lord, and not in us. We must trust God to lead them, and we must trust them to follow His instruction.

Specifically in missions, we must eliminate foolhardy strategies that grow from a misconception of the proper use of power. This misunderstanding arises primarily in two areas: people/staff and money. These are the areas we believe give power. We tend to say, "If we're going to pay and/or provide the personnel for it, we need to make the decisions."

I saw this early in my own ministry, when a missionary mentor led me to indigenize ministries in Europe. I did that very carefully over sixteen years, and we multiplied from a little work in Holland to the point of having 270 different types of ministries. These were drug rehabilitation centers, coffee houses, and even new churches. We had around 1,200 national workers, and nearly all of the ministry was being financially supported with national money. But to accomplish that, we as missionaries had to empower national leaders to learn some basic principles and then begin working it out in their own context.

3. Cooperative Networking and Partnership

We must move from a "stand-alone mentality" to cooperative networking and partnership. Most of us, especially in the Western world, seem to have developed a "stand-alone mentality." **If we say, "The Charismatic way of doing things is the only way that will work," we are positioning ourselves against what God is saying and doing today. The same is true if we say, "The non-Charismatic way of doing things is the only way that will work." It's equally true if we hold up our denomination or our missions agency, or our culture, as the only representative that speaks for God, has His mind and heart, and has His vision for ministry.** We must do away with arrogance and elitism that says, "Because we are who we are, we have something other people don't, and because of that, God is using us to the exclusion of others." As we throw away all pride, snobbery, and condescension, we will enter a new framework, which undergirds the servant mentality of networking to maximize strength and minimize weakness.

In that context, we must also step over cultural boundaries. As we empower national ministries, we will find that their strengths compliment ours. E. Stanley Jones, a famous Methodist missionary to India, recognized the truth of this concept many years ago when he noted,

The conception of one half of the world saved, and the other half lost, the half that is saved going out after the half lost, is a misconception. We are all lost without God. We are not only going to them because they are in need; we need what they can give to us. In the days to come, we shall want these men whose hearts have been touched with the grace of God to come and help us in the uncompleted task of evangelization.[15]

David Zac Niringui explains how that can happen when he describes a missions opportunity in his own nation of Uganda.

"Our church is just over 100 years old," he writes. "It has a rich history of Christian vitality and mission vision. It holds great potential for world missions." Still, he notes, "During the reign of Idi Amin in the 1970s Uganda had strong ties with Libya. Our governments had agreements to exchange personnel in various fields. Qualified Ugandans were free to apply for work in Libya. Doctors, nurses, engineers, and other technicians were invited to apply."

Did the Ugandan church seize the moment? "No," he reports. "In fact, some who were forced to go to Libya prayed day and night to come home. Meanwhile, Western mission agencies were praying for opportunities to send their people to Libya."

Niringui offers a haunting alternative. "Suppose our churches had been alert to this missionary opportunity," he says. "Church leaders could have encouraged our Christian professionals to apply for positions in Libya. If we had worked in partnership with Western agencies, they could have sent some Ugandans to Libya. None of this happened, because our Ugandan churches still thought of themselves as receiving churches and the Western churches as sending churches."[16]

What a sad story of a lost opportunity! Hopefully, we are at a point in the Christian world where we can learn from our mistakes and avoid repeating them. The Western Church propagated the kind of thinking Niringui describes. We must accept our responsibility in the matter and correct our mistakes. The eternal destiny of individuals, and indeed of entire cultures, depends on our ability to plant fully indigenous churches that will be self-governing, self-supporting, and self-propagating. But we also must teach them to look beyond themselves—to see their part in taking the gospel to all the peoples of the world. And then we must labor with them, as equal partners, to complete the task.

AIMS, a training, mobilizing, and networking agency which I have served as president, has built on this attitude as we have repeatedly established alliances and partnerships of churches, individuals, and agencies who are willing to reach over traditional barriers and labor together for a common goal. As I am writing this, our multiple alliances are altering the eternal future of people groups in the former Soviet Union, in China, in Africa, in Europe, in India, and in Asia. Participants come from a variety of doctrinal backgrounds, and they include many indigenous ministries.

Consider, for instance, our work in Ethiopia. In 1990, AIMS partnered with Calvary Temple in Denver, Colorado, and with the Evangelical Fellowship of Churches in Ethiopia (ECFE), which represents 97 percent of this nation's evangelical believers. Together, we trained and gave "startup support" to 313 national missionaries who came from twelve Ethiopian denominations. These believers already know the language, the customs, and the lifestyle. They are used to the diet. These highly motivated missionaries, whom I have met personally and consider to be among the best I've ever helped to train, are willing to give their lives for the sake of their countrymen's salvation. At that time, they pledged to target Ethiopia's sixty remaining unreached people groups, and they are enjoying incredible success. The new Joshua Project number is thirty-five, not sixty unreached people groups, and they are widening their vision to the nations that surround Ethiopia.

No single individual or group involved in this partnership could have seen these results by working alone. The simple fact is that a shared vision, a united effort, and a combination of resources always brings greater efficiency and power to accomplish specific tasks. As we reach across the superficial boundaries of history and culture, we will bring together synergistically the unique strengths God put within each individual, organization, and church, regardless of their geographic location or the culture in which they exist. The result will be an exponential multiplication in the harvest. This may be new and even threatening to some, but we are talking about the eternal destiny of millions of souls.

4. Positive Synergism

We must move from negative synergism to positive synergism. In the world of science, synergism occurs when someone puts two chemicals together, and their interaction produces a greater result together than would have happened if either had worked alone. God has a way of releasing new actions in the spiritual realm as well, and the purpose for those actions depends on us.

In Deuteronomy 32:30 we see an example of negative synergism:

How could one man chase a thousand, or two put ten thousand to flight, unless their Rock had sold them, unless the Lord had given them up?

God had given up on these people. He had quit giving them His wisdom and direction because they wouldn't listen. Now, their enemies were able to defeat them because of the synergistic effect of God's discipline and judgment in their midst.

On the other side of the coin, we see in Leviticus 26:8,

Five of you will chase a hundred, and a hundred of you will chase ten thousand, and your enemies will fall by the sword before you.

This verse shows God's people uniting as a team so that the results of their effort is multiplied by the results of positive synergism. Notice the mathematical power shift revealed in this verse. Certainly, Solomon understood this when he wrote,

Two are better than one, because they have a good return for their work: If one falls down, his friend can help him up. But pity the man who falls and has no one to help him up! Though one may be overpowered, two can defend themselves. A cord of three strands is not quickly broken. (Eccl. 4:9–12)

Once on an airplane, I talked to a professor from a large, well-respected university in the western U.S. He told me his department had conducted a study that demonstrated this same principle in the physical world. The researchers discovered that one horse could pull 9,000 pounds. They naturally thought two would pull 18,000 pounds. But when they checked their supposition and harnessed two horses together to see how much they could pull when working in partnership, they found the two horses together could actually pull 27,000 pounds. That is an example of the power of united effort as revealed in the natural world.

But the good news is, it's not limited to that realm. All churches and those in the missions community can experience a similar explosion of power to expand the borders of God's Kingdom, if we are willing to obey the principles of servanthood and if we are willing to lay aside our differences and move to a new level of positive synergism.

A Glimpse of a Strategic Power Shift in Attitude

"Let my heart be broken with what breaks God's heart." These words came from Dr. Bob Pierce, founder of World Vision, when he spoke in my home church just a few weeks after I was saved at the age of 19. Dr. Pierce gave a call to commitment for those willing to be a missionary. I wanted my heart broken, and even though I didn't understand what it meant to be a missionary, I responded. I cherish that moment and my missionary call. One of my life verses is:

> "Let my heart be broken with what breaks God's heart."

These are the ones I look on with favor: those who are humble and contrite in spirit, and who tremble at my word. (Isa. 66:2)

I believe that brokenness and humility are key attitudes to ministry.

A colleague of 35 years of ministry both in Teen Challenge and AIMS, Carolyn Hedgpeth, exudes this attitude. Our AIMS partnership with CBN/700 Club and Regent University was seeking a leader for a church-planting training center in Ukraine. I proposed that Carolyn take this position. She had the experience and education, but most of all, she had a servant's heart. This would be tested. She was appointed director. One hundred and ten men and women came for this training, many of whom were highly experienced in the underground church of the Soviet Union days. Some of the men did not accept the ministry of a woman teacher/

preacher. One was so anti-woman that he turned his chair around every time Carolyn taught, with his back facing her. Carolyn lovingly accepted him. Her broken and humble spirit won him over, and now they are close friends. He graduated the program and became a multiplying church planter.

Brokenness and humility reap eternal results where the arrogance of position fails.

Pause, Reflect, Pray, Plan

1.   Review the three Greek definitions of "serve" pp. 29-30.

2.   How does your ministry live up to these definitions? Write down what God tells you.

_____

_____

_____

_____

3.   Develop a plan to review these thoughts weekly for at least four to six weeks. Ask God to help you become an even better, habitual servant.

_____

_____

_____

_____

3

POWER SHIFT #2—ACTIONS

O. Henry, one of America's most beloved storytellers, had the unique ability to capture extraordinary meaning amid surprisingly ordinary circumstances. Writing in the early 1900s, he drew from his experiences, including a brief stint in prison, to write tales that exhibited tremendous compassion for the "common person." When he died in 1910, at the age of only forty-seven, he had been writing professionally for less than a decade. Yet he had firmly established himself as the most widely read storyteller in the nation.

One of O. Henry's most recognized stories is called "*The Gift of the Magi.*" It features a young married couple—Jim and Della Young. O. Henry described their meager circumstances, noting that they had only two possessions that stirred any pride—Jim's gold watch and Della's beautiful hair.

"Had the Queen of Sheba lived in the flat across the airshaft," O. Henry wrote, "Della would have let her hair hang out the window someday to dry just to depreciate Her Majesty's jewels and gifts. Had King Solomon been the janitor, with all his treasures piled up in the basement, Jim would have pulled out his watch every time he passed, just to see him pluck his beard in envy."

O. Henry opens this story with Della's dilemma—the next day will be Christmas, and she has only managed to save $1.87 to buy Jim's present. As the story proceeds, the author reveals that Della sells her precious hair to buy Jim a chain for his watch, and Jim sells his watch to buy Della some beautiful combs for her hair.

> "I love you" is an empty phrase without a demonstration of commitment and a willingness to sacrifice with some type of action.

O. Henry concludes, "...here I have lamely related to you the uneventful chronicle of two foolish children in a flat who most unwisely sacrificed for each other the greatest treasures of their house."[1] You see, Jim and Della are fictional characters who underscore one of life's great truths. They intuitively understood that words mean very little unless they are accompanied by action. **"I love you" is an empty phrase without a demonstration of commitment and a willingness to sacrifice with some type of action.**

This poignant story reflects the fact that "actions speak louder than words," a point which undergirds much of Scripture. The apostle John clearly indicated throughout his writings that love and obedience—attitude and action—must go hand in hand. He summarizes, "This is love for God: to obey his commands" (1 John 5:3a). And, of course, James reminds us, "As the body without the spirit is dead, so faith without deeds is dead" (Jas. 2:26).

All Four Strata of the Great Commission—Simultaneously!

God doesn't give commands without expecting our obedience, and the Great Commission is no exception. We know from Scripture that just before He ascended to heaven, Jesus gave His disciples specific instructions.

"But you will receive power when the Holy Spirit comes on you," He said, "and you will be my witnesses in Jerusalem, and in all Judea and Samaria, and to the ends of the earth" (Acts 1:8).

Let me say right up front that I believe this command is for all believers, even to the present day. I believe all Christians and all congregations are to be involved in some type of ministry in their locality, in their nation, in neighboring nations, and in the spiritual frontiers of this earth. And I believe this ministry is to happen simultaneously— we don't have to win everyone at home before we step out of our own neighborhoods.

The Jerusalem Church may have understood that, but their actions didn't show it. They experienced God's power, as revealed in Acts 2, but they didn't move very far out of their cultural comfort zone. Certainly, on the day of Pentecost, people from all over the world heard the gospel. But outside of that preliminary evangelistic thrust, the Jerusalem Church did little to push the gospel outside the limits of its own city.

Don Richardson has even gone so far as to express, "Hundreds of millions of Christians think that Luke's Acts of the Apostles records the 12 apostles' obedience to the Great Commission. Actually, it records their reluctance to obey it." He notes that they quickly evangelized Jerusalem at Pentecost and in the days that immediately followed, so that Acts 5:28 records the apostles' critics complaining, "You have filled Jerusalem with your teaching." Still, Richardson adds, "Twenty-five percent of the book of Acts was already history, and as far as the record shows, they were not even making plans to obey the rest of Jesus' command."[2]

This Jerusalem congregation was on the verge of sectarianism until some laypeople went out and planted a church in Antioch. And then, when the leaders of the Jerusalem Church heard about it, they convened a council. If this council had not allowed God to break through, something would have happened to this church. I believe they would have died on the vine. God didn't need them to finish His mission—just like He doesn't need your church or my church. He'll scoot around us and go fulfill His plan, whether we go with Him or not. But we will miss the great joy that comes with obedience—the joy of knowing that we have pleased and honored our Father.

At any rate, this council met to discuss a spiritual beachhead established among the Gentiles in Antioch. Based on his own experience in cross-cultural ministry, Simon Peter supported this outreach. Barnabas and

Paul, who were reporting on behalf of the believers in Antioch, described what was happening there. And finally, James, also supporting this new endeavor, quoted an Old Testament prophecy:

After this I will return and re-build David's fallen tent. Its ruins I will rebuild, and I will restore it, that the remnant of men may seek the Lord, and all the Gentiles who hear my name, says the Lord, who does these things' that have been known for ages. (Acts 15:16–18, quoting Amos 9:11–12)

According to this passage, God's tent is being built prophetically. The tabernacle was the place where God disclosed Himself. It revealed the presence of God in the Kingdom of God, which in the end time is the restored Body of Christ. "After this I will return," God said, referring to the outpouring of the Holy Spirit. That outpouring leads to rebuilding and restoring the tent. And restoration leads to the *ethne*—that is, people from all ethnic groups—seeking the Lord.

The typology here is obvious. Israel was to dispossess all nations and take possession of the land God had given them. Our responsibility is to dispossess the powers of our spiritual enemy, Satan, and take control of the nations. I believe He wants us to do that by being knowledgeable and mindful of solid, strategic principles in establishing a church-planting movement in every people group.

Admittedly, this is a daunting task. But as author Horace Fenton explained in *Myths about Missions,*

It all comes down to this: Either Christ was deceived in believing that the job can be done, or we have been deceived in believing that it cannot. Knowing full well our own capacity for being deceived, we should be able to easily accept the fact that what we have believed is a myth, while Christ has been utterly trustworthy, as always.[3]

So, when we think the task is overwhelming, let's keep in mind that in both Amos 9:12 and Acts 15:17, God refers to "all the Gentiles (*ethne* in the Greek) who bear my name." Based on those passages, we can see that all people groups are dedicated to His name. That means there are people out there in Brunei and Bhutan and all the unreached areas of the earth who, if they would receive the message of the gospel, they would immediately respond. That's my conviction. If we took the gospel to everybody on earth who had never heard it before, we'd have such a harvest that we wouldn't be able to contain it. In every *ethne*, people are waiting to experience the love of Jesus.

So, the underlying implication for this passage, in context with Acts 1:8 as well, is that **God wanted His followers to understand why He gave the Holy Spirit—it was for the purpose of action. The Holy Spirit's coming is intended to empower believers for expanding the borders of God's Kingdom all over the world.** By containing it in our own cultural framework, we disobey God. When the Jerusalem Church saw this, they experienced a tremendous power shift that enabled them to minister as Christ intended—in Jerusalem, Judea, Samaria, and to the ends of the earth.

Historic Missions: From Cross-Cultural to Indigenization

Throughout history, those involved in missions have experienced power shifts like that described in Scripture for the Church at Jerusalem. As I mentioned in the previous chapter, even the great Reformation of the 16th century, which gave birth to Protestant Christianity, did not launch any real missions zeal. As Ruth Tucker explains in her landmark book *From Jerusalem to Irian Jaya: A Biographical History of Christian Missions*, Protestants were doing their best to just hold their own against Roman Catholic opposition. They did not have a ready-made mission force. But also, their theology stood in the way of cross-cultural ministry.

"Martin Luther was so certain of the imminent return of Christ that he overlooked the necessity of foreign missions," Tucker notes. He also believed the Great Commission was binding only on the first-century apostles. Calvinists followed a similar argument, but they also believed the doctrine of election eliminated or at least reduced the need for foreign missions since "God had already chosen those he would save."[4]

Among Protestants, it wasn't until the 1700s that the Moravians, William Carey, and a few others began to see what God has always seen and felt for those who have never heard the gospel. They pushed from a level of inactivity to becoming involved among the people groups who lived on the continental coastlands. The next missionary assault, led by people like David Livingstone and Hudson Taylor, pushed from the coastlands to the interior, strategically targeting hidden people groups.

Now we know who the unreached *ethne* are—at least we know a lot of them. We can discover them by becoming familiar with the country listings of unreached people groups on *joshuaproject.net*. Differences in definition yield differences in research results, so that **Jim Reapsome** once wrote in his column in *Evangelical Mission Quarterly*,

What's the only uncontested truth about unreached peoples? (1) They are eternally lost without Christ, and (2) we are supposed to reach them with the gospel as eagerly as the apostle Paul set his sights on Rome. *All other "truths" about these people—exactly who they are and how we should reach them—are simply the best of our human diagnostics and prescriptions.*[5]

He has a point, but the bottom line is that for many unreached peoples, we do know the answers to the crucial questions of who, what, when, why, and how to reach them. We know the languages they speak. We know their geopolitical boundaries. We know if they're living in an open country or a closed country. We're beginning to understand different strategies for reaching them. We have seen a massive power shift from general missions on the coastlands, to targeting the interior, and finally to directing our energies toward the unreached people groups. The result will be the completion of Christ's final mandate, the Great Commission, as we strategically take the gospel to every people group in the world.

We also are moving away from a paradigm that allows for "dead-end missions" as we continually see the value of partnering with laborers in the Two-thirds World. I define "dead-end missions" as those endeavors that don't indigenize the work by encouraging and training nationals to assume responsibility for the ministry and even to send out their own missionaries.

> I define "dead-end missions" as those endeavors that don't indigenize the work by encouraging and training nationals to assume responsibility for the ministry and even to send out their own missionaries.

The comments from one African brother underline this point. Pius Wakatama stated that he felt no restrictions should be placed on legitimate missionaries who have a burden to win Africans with the gospel. He added,

However, I feel equally strongly that all restrictions should be placed on missionaries coming to Africa to do work that can be done by Africans. We need only those missionaries who are qualified and willing to train Africans for responsibility. There is no longer room for missionaries who will come to work as directors without Timothys at their side who will eventually take over for them. Such missionaries will never be out of work because Africa has millions of Timothys waiting to be trained in order to train others.[6]

Unfortunately, though this African brother issued that warning in 1976, many missionaries and mission organizations still have not taken to heart these words, which represent the feelings of millions of people all over the world. After all, it all comes down to respect and trust in God to work in His people.

I visited a Bible school on another continent run by three American missionaries, each with master's degrees in missiology from American seminaries. They had 300 students at their school, and there were many unreached people groups within their own nation. I asked the nationals who were studying there, "What about these unreached people groups?" Their answer was heartbreaking. "That's what we have American missionaries for," they said. That school didn't have a single missions course in its curriculum. I call that a "dead-end" mission.

> Watch out for the "black hole" of funding people and projects that don't produce fruit for the Kingdom.

Our goal must be to teach every church and every believer throughout the world to be involved in evangelism at the local level and in cross-cultural ministry as well, even to the spiritual frontiers where the gospel has not yet penetrated. The bottom line is that the Two-thirds World is currently producing more missionaries than the West is. We must recognize that trend and use it for God's glory. That means we must move away from supporting "dead-end" missions. **Watch out for the "black hole" of funding people and projects that don't produce fruit for the Kingdom.**

What Does That Mean for the Future?

Given this historical understanding of power shifts that are impacting missionary outreach even to the present day, it's important that we examine God's purposes and determine additional corrections He wants to encourage for the purpose of multiplying the results of our efforts throughout the world. My research and experience have led me to note five power shifts that I believe God wants to work in our midst.

1. Holistic Cooperation

We must move from local church/parachurch competition to holistic cooperation. Christ did not intend for His Bride to be at war with herself. He has a role for each individual, each congregation, and each missions agency to play, and it's a cooperative role—not a competitive one. As **John R.W. Stott reminds us,**

> **The responsibilities which God has entrusted to his Church, he has entrusted to his whole Church ... God's people ... are both a**

priestly people, to offer him the acceptable, spiritual sacrifices of praise and prayer, and a missionary people to declare to others the excellences of their God.[7]

Stott goes on to note the biblical use of the word *koinonia*, which we have translated fellowship, as "more than what we share *in* together. There is also, and secondly, what we share *out* together. For *koinonia* in the New Testament concerns not only what we possess but what we *do* together, not only our common inheritance but also our common service." Stott points out that "Luke uses *koinonia* to describe the business relationship between the pairs of brothers, James and John, Andrew and Simon." In effect, Luke uses this word to mean "partners, colleagues, engaged in the fishing trade." Paul uses the same word to refer to his co-laborers Titus and Philemon. He also uses it when he refers to the Philippian Christians as his "partners in the gospel."[8]

Thus, fellowship in the body of Christ takes on an entirely new meaning. It's not just Saturday night's fellowship meeting. It's also partnership for the sake of spreading the gospel. And it's crucial that we come to understand this if we are truly serious about completing the Great Commission anytime soon. **It's a power shift we can't afford to miss.**

Consider, for example, the results that could be accomplished for God's Kingdom if a group of churches and agencies targeted an unreached people group in a desert region. Suppose a national church could provide missionaries. Two or three western churches could provide funding and training. An agency agrees to dig wells. Another provides projectors and screens for the missionaries. Another provides the Jesus film. Another provides Bibles and follow-up literature.

Once the wells are dug, they become the social hub for the region. The national missionary shows the Jesus film there and provides Bibles and discipleship materials. He or she meets with the group of converts on a regular basis and teaches them the principles of multiplication. In a brief time, these individuals and churches and agencies have established a self-replicating church planting movement within an unreached people group, and then they are free to move to another group. These kinds of results, though, are only possible in an atmosphere where actions demonstrate an atmosphere of cooperation rather than competition.

2. Missions-Mobilized Churches

We must move from inactive churches to missions-mobilized churches. I truly believe that God desires to reach the world by using local churches. I agree with the man who referred to a series of meetings involving Christian leaders from many different countries who met to discuss the task of evangelizing the world. "In each place," Horace L. Fenton noted, "there had been a frank recognition of the enormous dimensions of the task. This was something to be done not just by a spiritual elite called 'missionaries,' or a similarly gifted group called 'national pastors.' The task of total evangelism would not be accomplished merely by multiplying the numbers of these two groups." The author goes on to say the answer is in mobilizing "every member of the church" to be involved in the task.[9]

Several years ago, I took a trip to Africa with representatives from American and Canadian churches who had recognized their responsibility for reaching the world. We had partnered them with a new African Bible school about to graduate their first 12 students. The questions in the North Americans' minds were, "Are these people effectively penetrating unreached people groups with the gospel? Should we support them?" Here's what happened.

The African leader and his students heard rumors of a tribe that lived in the bush in their nation, but they weren't sure the group even really existed. This tribe apparently had never been contacted. It was on no database. They agreed to send representatives to check out the rumor, and that group hiked three days into the bush. Suddenly, they were surrounded by tribal people armed with poisoned arrows and spears. They were taken captive for two days and, though they were unable to communicate with anyone, they did, however, meet the chief.

Eventually, they were released, but God had placed a burden on their hearts, and they began praying for their countrymen in the bush. They felt a distinct need to return, and they found a language interpreter who was willing to go with them. They were taken prisoner again and were taken to the chief, but this time they were able to witness to him. As a result, he and his entire village believed in Jesus, and the group of students was able to plant a church there.

"How many people are in your whole tribe?" they asked the chief. The students were surprised to learn there were probably thousands more people in this group, and before their visit, no one in the Bible school even knew for sure they existed. Here's what they discovered. Within one month, these African students were instrumental in planting 70 more house churches in that tribe. What an example to follow that resulted in a tremendous breakthrough!

We need to establish certain kinds of churches if we are to accomplish these types of results. At AIMS, we've established a checklist of six criteria that we believe should be the target for any church who truly wishes to be mobilized for missions. Carefully and prayerfully consider these following criteria of a missions-mobilized church.

1. This church should engage in faithful, committed, and informed intercession on behalf of the whole world, and also on behalf of at least one adopted unreached people group.

2. This church should be raising resources to fuel and fund the Great Commission movement. Translated into raw numbers, we believe at least 10 percent of the church's total budget should be earmarked for cross-cultural ministry. At least one-fourth of that amount, or 2.5 percent of the church's total budget, should go specifically to target unreached people groups. Some churches, of course, choose to do more, but we believe this should be the minimum. How can we do more? Every church should teach faith promise giving. This is the teaching and process that enabled the People's Church in

Toronto, Canada, to develop a missions budget of 50% of their total revenue.

3.   This church should strive to engage at least 10 percent of its adult attendees in some type of cross-cultural ministry. This may include short-term trips, lifestyle evangelism with international students, etc.

4.   This church should strive to engage at least 1 to 2 percent of its adults as career missionaries and/or tentmakers. Remember, Christ told us to ask the Lord of the Harvest to send out laborers. It seems that the best place to begin is by asking Him to call them forth from among our own congregations.

5.   This church should help other churches become mobilized for missions. They pass their vision along to other church leaders and enlist other churches in the task of building God's Kingdom throughout the world through cooperative endeavors.

6.   This church should network and partner with international, indigenous churches, organizations, and individuals in the global Great Commission community.

3. Strategic Churches

We must move from reactive churches to strategic churches. Reactive churches prefer the status quo. Fenton described these churches like this:

> **In the realm of thought as well as of action our theme song often seems to be "Come abundance or come woe, my status is quo."** *We resist change everywhere, and nowhere more than in the realm of long-cherished ideas. Result: We think wrongly and often unbiblically. We become the victims of our own myths. All*

unconsciously, **we have married our myths to God's truth,** *and it is time we put asunder what man has joined together.*[10]

In reactive churches, if they change their program at all, they generally choose to simply adopt programs that were successful elsewhere. They are consistently in a reactive rather than proactive posture, surprised by events and by twists and turns in circumstances.

Strategic churches, on the other hand, are planning for closure of the Great Commission. They hold the goal of reaching the world for Christ to be a priority command, not just a suggestion. For instance, they might choose to give a larger portion of their budget to a missionary working among the unreached than to someone working in an area with local churches that have already been evangelized.

4. Missionaries with Specialized Skills

We must move from fostering general missionaries to fostering specialized missionaries. Don't just send willing "warm bodies" to foreign countries. Encourage people to train for specialized ministry. Then enable them to go somewhere else and train a national to do a specific ministry task. Our end goal should be to put ourselves out of business. For instance, I don't recommend that a church send more church planters to Brazil, where the church is already relatively strong. But you may want to consider sending someone who can train Brazilians in various specialized ministries, like local church missions mobilization. Then, when that specialized ministry is indigenized, the missionaries retrain for another specialized ministry or move to another country needing their expertise. In this mobilization process, the Brazilian churches would adopt all the unreached people groups in their country, and even beyond, with an end vision to help complete the Great Commission.

5. Expand into New People Groups

We must move from expecting growth only in existing outreaches to expansion within new groups. Statistics indicate that, even if revival broke out in every church in the world, and if that revival never went beyond the cultures that already have churches, then 3.14 billion people would still go without the gospel. Revival is not the only answer. Revival needs to produce equippers who understand God's strategy. It is especially important that we also send missionaries to regions and to people groups where there is no church. We must preach in Jerusalem, but also to the ends of the earth, among people who have not heard God wooing them into a relationship with Him.

The Old Testament prophet Jonah tried to refuse God's direct order regarding cross-cultural ministry, and he experienced severe discipline. If we refuse to reach out in all directions, taking God's love to our neighbors and to the darkest regions of the world, then we can expect the same type of "training." But even beyond the desire to avoid discipline, if we spurn our Lord's direct command, we will disappoint our Father. And that, in itself, should be the motivation for our obedience.

A Glimpse of a Strategic Power Shift in Action

I remember the day when Michael Little, then president of CBN/700 Club told me; "Howard, we have twelve to thirteen million names of people in the Soviet Union who prayed to receive Jesus Christ at the end of our "Superbook" program." He went on to say, "You're a church planter. Can these names be used to plant churches?" We put together a partnership of over one hundred American churches working with Soviet churches that were emerging from the underground. Soviet and American pastors joined together in doing evangelistic rallies with the names obtained from the CBN broadcast from all over the Soviet Union. This was a partnership of AIMS, CBN, and Regent University to serve the Soviet church that was rising out of persecution and oppressive government control.

This servant-oriented action planted nearly 500 churches that also grew into over 40,000 cell groups. What a partnership! This dramatic surge of church planting helped open all the various Soviet regions to the gospel.

Pause, Reflect, Pray, Plan

1.   How is your church doing in terms of the six criteria on pp 53-54?

2.   List three to four actions you could take to help your church power shift to a more fruitful and strategic posture.

     _____

     _____

     _____

     _____

3.   Develop a time line of action steps to apply the power shift principles to your personal life.

     _____

     _____

     _____

     _____

4

POWER SHIFT #3—ALIGNMENT

Possibly you are familiar with the story of a certain naval battleship group that was out at sea. It's been told repeatedly, with various alterations in details, but here's the version that came across our humor network at the AIMS office. It's supposedly the transcript of an actual radio conversation between a naval ship off the coast of Newfoundland and the Canadian authorities who monitor the region.

Naval ship: Please divert your course 15 degrees to the North to avoid a collision.

Canadians: Recommend you divert YOUR course 15 degrees to the South to avoid a collision.

Naval ship: This is the Captain of a Navy ship. I say again, divert YOUR course.

Canadians: No. I say again, you divert YOUR course.

Naval ship: THIS IS AN AIRCRAFT CARRIER. WE ARE ACCOMPANIED BY THREE DESTROYERS, THREE CRUISERS, AND NUMEROUS SUPPORT VESSELS. I DEMAND THAT YOU CHANGE YOUR COURSE 15 DEGREES TO THE NORTH, OR COUNTER-MEASURES WILL BE UNDERTAKEN TO ENSURE THE SAFETY OF THIS SHIP.

Canadians: This is a lighthouse. Your call.

The story generally produces a chuckle. Obviously, the lighthouse's purpose was to provide direction, and only an arrogant fool would ignore it. Yet many of us choose to ignore the Light of the World. Even if we answer His call to take the gospel to the world, too often, we choose to do it our way instead of His. We need to adjust our priorities and strategies so they line up with His. Many of us need a shift in our alignment.

Quit Looking for the Payoff

The Great Commission says we are to go to all peoples—not just to the responsive ones. Western culture has taught us to look for immediate returns and results. We want a big payoff for our missions investment, but most of us aren't willing to wait.

If John Nevius had held this attitude, he never would have gone to Seoul, Korea, in 1890.[1] Though Protestant missionaries were seeing some success in Korea at that time, it was still a hard field. It had only been about thirty years since Roman Catholic missionaries had experienced extreme hostility. But Nevius, a veteran Presbyterian missionary with experience in China, implemented the beginning of the indigenous church movement that we know today. If it hadn't been for Nevius, who went there and wrestled through spiritual warfare and paid the price when it was a resistant field, we wouldn't have the Korean revival and church growth we see today. *Operation World* says that South Korea is over 20% Evangelical, and other sources go as high as one-third. **What a powerful testimony of the Spirit-led power of alignment!**

The Great Commission is all about obedience—not results, but biblical obedience brings results. Some church growth theorists say we should go only to the ripe fields. But someone must clear the fields, plow the ground, and spread the fertilizer before the harvest comes. We have tremendous indigenous outreach in Korea today because Nevius and others plowed the ground. They took those tree stumps out and tossed the rocks aside, and through their obedience to God, they made a receptive field out of Korea.

That could happen in many other parts of the world today if we would do what Nevius did. **We must experience a shift in our alignment. We** must come to understand that without raising up and supporting pioneer missionaries who will go to the difficult areas of the world and proclaim the Gospel, perhaps laboring for years before they see results, we will never complete the Great Commission.

That process begins with prayer and spiritual warfare on behalf of those who live in closed countries. It then progresses with a willingness to move in obedience when God realigns our strategies, redirects our energies, and provides a *kairos* moment.

What Is a Kairos Moment?

Bruce Larson's book, *Living Out the Book of Acts*, explains that Scripture uses two different words to refer to time, *chronos* and *kairos*. The first, *chronos*, refers to time that we measure with calendars and clocks. This is the root word for our term "chronology." Larson explains,

That's one kind of time, and if we think we have only that dimension, we end up being what doctors call Type A personalities, driven workaholics prone to cardiovascular problems and heart attacks. Most of us are all too aware that we've got only so much measurable time, so we get up earlier and work harder to accomplish our goals.[2]

But there is another kind of time, Larson reminds us, and in Greek, it's called *kairos*. This term is translated "in the fullness of time" or "the moment of opportunity." In effect, a *kairos* moment is that special time when God sets all the details in order and blows open the door, and then He gives us the opportunity to go along with Him in what He's about to accomplish. Larson notes that Jesus lived and ministered on *kairos* time, and He commanded His disciples to do

> In effect, a kairos moment is that special time when God sets all the details in order and blows open the door, and then He gives us the opportunity to go along with Him in what He's about to accomplish.

the same. In Acts 1:8 we read, "You shall receive power and you will be my witnesses." Larson explains,

> *The disciples were to act on the kairos principle. After Jesus' ascension, they went back to the Upper Room where they had celebrated the Last Supper with Him and there they waited. They could accomplish nothing until the power came. When the kairos comes, you're on God's agenda; the door opens and you go through it and give it all you've got.*[3]

Paul experienced that kind of divine intervention when he headed for Asia. Acts 16 tells us the Holy Spirit kept him from preaching there, and then He realigned Paul's target area when he gave the apostle a vision of a Macedonian man seeking spiritual help. Church history reveals that other apostles and missionaries went to Asia. God didn't leave them languishing without the gospel message, as evidenced by the fact that all seven Revelation churches were in the province of Asia. But God had a specific task for Paul and his team, and it was not in Asia but in Europe.

Implications for Today's Great Commission Community

Paul's experience represents a power shift in missions in the first century. As we enter the 21st century, we need to learn the same lesson Paul did—we need to recognize that God has an overall plan for the evangelization of the world, and He has specific roles for every church and every individual believer and every missions agency. As we align ourselves with His strategy and fulfill the role He has assigned to us, we will see that, by His sovereignty, He will use each of us to bring closure to the Great Commission.

In my experience and through my study, I have come to see eight areas where the contemporary missions community must examine itself to ensure compliance with and obedience to God's perfect will.

1. Obey God's Revealed Will

We must move from only human planning to revealed direction. As we noted previously, Paul experienced this. Human planning told him to go to Asia. It was the logical thing to do. The Holy Spirit revealed something entirely different.

We cannot do missions based on nothing more than a good business plan. We need spiritual revelation to understand God's plan and His timing. Only within that framework can we truly expect miraculous results and exponential increase.

This may be a little controversial, but I believe Jonah is one of the best Old Testament examples of this. The book that bears his name opens with this statement:

"The word of the Lord came to Jonah son of Amittai:

"Go to the great city of Nineveh and preach against it, because its wickedness has come up before me" (Jonah 1:1–2).

God gave a specific task to this Hebrew man, and as you know, he disobeyed and endured God's corrective discipline in the form of a big fish that swallowed him up. At the very end of chapter two, we find that, when Jonah repented of his sin, God caused the fish to vomit him up on shore. Then chapter three starts right off with this statement.

Then the word of the Lord came to Jonah a second time: "Go to the great city of Nineveh and proclaim to it the message I give you." (Jonah 3:1–2)

God gave clear instructions, and Jonah rediscovered his *kairos* moment. Of course, he wasn't too pleased about it, but he obeyed. He marched into the great city and issued the Old Testament equivalent of a "turn or burn" message—not exactly a new, an innovative, or the best strategy—but the people responded. Scripture tells us, "When God saw what they [the Ninevites] did and how they turned from their evil ways, he had compassion and did not bring on them the destruction he had threatened" (Jonah 3:10).

Sometimes the *kairos* moment depends on our waiting, as in the case of the disciples who waited in the Upper Room after Jesus' ascension. Sometimes it depends on our moving ahead in obedience, as it did with Jonah. But always it depends on our hearing from God and moving according to His revealed direction. As **Andrew Murray** once explained, **"All that the Church and its members need for the manifestation of the mighty power of God in the world is the return to our true place, the place of absolute and unceasing dependence upon God."**[4]

2. Provide Spontaneity within Structure

> Structure by itself will never implement the dynamic of the Spirit, but it certainly can impede it.

We must move from a rigid structure to spontaneity. Please understand, I'm not suggesting that we do away with structure altogether. Structure is like a skeleton—it should support but not inhibit activity. **Structure by itself will never implement the dynamic of the Spirit, but it certainly can impede it.** You can have a great organization. It can be put together as effectively as the human body. But if it's not receiving the messages from the Head—Jesus Christ—then the structure is only getting in the way of what God wants to accomplish.

We must be careful with man-made structures, always laying them before the Lord and being willing to adjust to meet the needs of the moment. A mission leader from India explains, "If I were to claim that the Model T Ford was the greatest method of transportation of all time, I doubt anyone would take me seriously. True, in its day, the Model T was on the cutting edge of technology. We look admiringly back to this point in transportation history, but that day is over. You and I realize this, and we've moved ahead with the times to faster and more efficient ways of getting around."[5] Yet, he points out, many missions organizations are still clinging to their own personal Model Ts in the forms of structures and outdated strategies. This may require some tough, but necessary decisions.

This leader is right: structure and strategy make great servants but lousy masters. Certainly, I'm not saying we should be totally spontaneous— that would be ridiculous. But I believe we should be ready, like the mobile team Paul had, to change our plans when God directs us in a different way.

One of my friends is the head of a mission board with about 1800 missionaries on the field. When the Iron Curtain crumbled and the former Soviet Union was suddenly open for ministry, he sent a letter to all his missionaries and said, "If you can possibly train a replacement or leave what you're doing and go to the former Soviet Union, do it." That's an example of spontaneity within structure. Certainly, we must have structure, but we must keep it flexible and not allow it to get in the way of the Holy Spirit's movement.

3. Target People Groups, Not Countries

We must move from targeting countries to targeting people groups. When Christ told His followers to take the gospel to all nations, He used the word *ethne*. In Greek, that means "peoples." It's the basis for the English word "ethnic." In terms of missions strategy, categorizing the task of world evangelization in terms of people groups gives a much clearer picture of what remains to be done.

For example, the nation of India could never be adequately targeted as an entire country. It's a virtual mosaic of cultures and languages, and every one of the 1600 unreached people groups in this nation demand and deserves a unique strategy for their evangelization. One plan may have worked remarkably well among Muslims in Indonesia, but that doesn't mean it will work at all among Muslims of Northern India. We must pray and find God's unique solution for each people group. **We need to realize that targeting people groups is the basic, biblical strategy. It came from the mouth and heart of Jesus, "Go and make disciples of all nations (*ethne*)" (Mt. 28:19)**

4. Participate in God's Big Picture

We must move from seeing only our exclusive part to seeing the inclusive whole of missions work. As I noted earlier in this chapter, God has a specific plan for each Christian and for each church, but He also has an overarching plan that will bring about the completion of the Great Commission. We must never forget that God is calling other people to do other things in other places.

Adoption is a perfect example of this. Many mission organizations, AIMS included, encourage churches, families, individuals, small cell groups, etc. to focus their mission efforts by adopting an unreached people group. The adopting body seeks God's wisdom and direction and then "adopts" an unreached people group. Participants agree to pray for that group, and in the AIMS model, they go so far as to commit resources (time, money, and personnel) for the purpose of helping to establish a church-planting movement among their adopted people group.

So, here's the bottom line. Suppose the First Church of Houston, Texas, with a congregation of about 5,000, adopts the Hausa of Nigeria. So does the First Church of Burlington, Vermont, with a congregation of 200. The Texas church may have tremendous wealth and resources, while the Vermont church has little in the way of funds. However, it does have a unique resource—Hausa international students attend a local college. If these churches have a grasp of the "big picture" for winning their adopted people group, they will accomplish much more by working together than either could accomplish by working alone.

I believe future mission work will be exponentially multiplied as the Church, in general, experiences this power shift. As we begin to see how our calling fits the total picture, we will be able to work cooperatively with others for the sake of those who have yet to hear God's good news in a way they can understand.

For the "how to" of adopting unreached people groups, see the AIMS website at <u>www.aims.org</u>.

5. Vision – Complete the Great Commission

We must move from being involved only in missions activity to being strategically involved in bringing about closure, or the completion of the Great Commission. I have told this story in other books and publications, but it's such a great example, I hope you will bear with me while I run through it again. When my two sons were young, my wife Pat and I served as missionaries in Europe. Pat often tells of a morning when she sat at a table, working and "keeping an eye" on the boys at the same time. They were playing together, squatting down like sprinters, and the older boy would say, "Go!" They would race around and around the table until he would say, "Fall down!" Then both boys would "hit the deck," panting and dizzy.

They repeated this game over and over until she finally asked, "What are you doing?"

"It's a game we made up," they said. "We call it 'missionary.'"

The story always brings a chuckle, but the sad truth is my sons were offering an effective commentary on missions-as-we-know-it. Traditional missions endeavors, while they have introduced many to the gospel, have also failed to release almost half of the world's population from Satan's strongholds. In a sense, those who insist on maintaining traditional missions are running in circles without much to show for their effort, in terms of completing the Great Commission. They've spent a lot of time and money and effort, but they haven't been strategic.

In business or education or any secular venture, we readily see the importance of establishing goals and objectives. They guide our activities by helping us prioritize needs and responses. The same must be true for the Great Commission community. Our activities must be planned and supported with a view of completing the Great Commission—that is establishing God's Kingdom in every people group in the world. Closure (i.e., completing the Great Commission) must be our overall objective and measurable, observable goals need to be evidenced as we move forward.

6. Employ Cultural Research

We must move from assumptions to research. I noted in an earlier chapter the need for missionaries to have adequate training for cross-cultural ministry. That includes education in language, cross-cultural communication, etc. But the preparation can't end there—not even for the local church here in the United States that's supporting that missionary.

A wealth of information is available regarding almost every people group on earth. You can discover their language, geo-political boundaries, religious orientation, family structure, diet, etc. Access to facts such as these not only prepares the missionary, but it also enables supporting individuals and churches to pray effectively. Research is an incredible tool for the expansion of God's Kingdom throughout the world. **AIMS primarily uses the Joshua Project database, www.joshuaproject.net. Do yourself a favor and learn about the resources there.**

7. Establish Self-Replicating Churches

We must move from witnessing only to discipling and church planting. Crusades and numbers don't matter if we don't leave behind mature believers and churches who are able to continue the work. When the former Soviet Union first opened its doors to Christians, Moscow's ten million people had only fifty Protestant churches. Several big-name evangelists went in and did crusades, at which they claimed that thousands of people went forward to receive Christ as their Savior. But some of them didn't plant churches to conserve the harvest, and the work died when they left. If your calling is to evangelize and witness and win converts only, then please, please network with others who are planting churches. We must establish self-replicating churches and church planting movements if we ever intend to see lasting results.

8. Maximize the Harvest

We must move from a mechanical, business paradigm to an agricultural paradigm. The mechanical view leads us to go only where we see immediate results. It leads us to give where we get the "biggest bang for our buck"—where we'll see the quickest return on our investment—where we'll see the largest numbers of "souls saved." The agricultural paradigm, on the other hand, will not allow us to forget about the 40 percent of the world that is still hard and infertile that needs, and indeed requires, initial cultivation.

The prophet Isaiah stayed within the agricultural framework when he gave the Lord's specific instruction.

Listen and hear my voice," God said. "Pay attention and hear what I say. When a farmer plows for planting, does he plow continually? Does he keep on breaking up and harrowing the soil? When he has leveled the surface, does he not sow caraway and scatter cumin? Does he not plant wheat in its place, barley in its plot, and spelt in its field? His God instructs him and teaches him the right way (Isa. 28:23–26).

Let me offer a few observations from this passage. First, there is a time for preparing the field, and if it's never been farmed before, this stage is a lengthy process. The farmer cuts down trees and removes stumps and digs out rocks. Then he plows and breaks up the ground, then harrows and levels it out. His goal is to prepare the soil so it will accept the seed and yield the greatest harvest possible. And when the soil is ready, it's time to quit plowing.

In missions, this process involves strategic prayer and intercession. It requires sending pioneer missionaries, as we noted earlier in this chapter. And it means that we don't necessarily expect immediate results. Harvest will come, in due time, but only if we persevere in this season of clearing out obstacles and preparing people to accept the Word of our Lord by developing good and receptive soil.

Second, different kinds of seeds do better in different kinds of soil. If you plant wheat in the plot that was intended for barley, you will diminish your yield. The same is true in missions—different kinds of seeds (methods) work better in different kinds of soil. And if you apply an inappropriate strategy, you limit your yield. That's where research comes in—you need to know what kind of seed to plant in your specific field. Missions is not a "cookie cutter" endeavor.

But the passage doesn't end there, for it also describes the harvest.

Caraway is not threshed with a sledge," Isaiah wrote, "nor is a cartwheel rolled over cumin; caraway is beaten out with a rod, and cumin with a stick. Grain must be ground to make bread; so one does not go on threshing it forever. Though he drives the wheels of his threshing cart over it, his horses do not grind it. All this also comes from the LORD Almighty, wonderful in counsel and magnificent in wisdom." (Isa. 28:27–29)

The spiritual parallel here is that God gives directions in how to reap a spiritual harvest because successful strategies vary in different cultures and with different generations.

Both sections of this passage offer the reassurance that God gives wisdom regarding how the farmer is to proceed in each situation—reaping as well as sowing. And the bottom line, in both the physical and the spiritual realm, is that you never sow seed as an end in itself. You always intend to get a harvest. And your goal is to get the maximum harvest by planting the appropriate seed for that kind of soil; this is a "unique solution" approach.

"There is a time for everything," Scripture reminds us, **"A time to be born and a time to die, a time to plant and a time to uproot" (Eccl. 3:1-2)**. Also, Genesis 8:22 states, **"As long as the earth endures, <u>seedtime and harvest</u>, cold and heat, summer and winter, day and night will never cease."**

Only as we replace the mechanical business paradigm with this agricultural paradigm will we understand the importance of each step in the process. Preparing the soil is just as important as taking in the harvest, even though it tests our patience, our zeal, and our commitment.

But remember—the Great Commission is not just about immediate results. It's about obedience.

A Glimpse of a Strategic Power Shift in Alignment

"Howard, there's a call from Mark Buntain in Calcutta." This statement came from my secretary in our Eurasia Teen Challenge office in Germany. Missionary Buntain asked, "Can you help us open a Teen Challenge ministry in Calcutta?"

Three months later, I landed at the Calcutta airport. My plane was delayed, and there was no one to meet me. (This was before smartphones). I found an English-speaking taxi driver and took off for Hotel Hindustan. It was a long drive, and even at 6 a.m., there were masses of people on the streets, and some were obviously living on the sidewalks. Children, drawn by my white face, knocked on the taxi windows at the stoplights, begging for food. I gave all my Indian money away.

In my hotel room, I fell on my face in prayer before God. "Father, if you can use me here, please anoint and help me." The phone rang. It was the church, "We have a tour for you." The next day, I was taken to Mother Teresa's House of the Destitute and Dying. Over one hundred street people were lying on pallets, waiting to die. Catholic nuns lovingly tended to them. The next stop was a funeral pyre next to a river. They were burning the bodies of street people who died the previous night. The guide from the church said, "We have about one million people living on the streets and the garbage dumps." Third, we went to the Temple of Cali, a Hindu Goddess. "They sometimes sacrifice children here," I was told. My heart was broken. I went back to the hotel to prepare to preach that night. My heart was heavy with the immensity of the need.

God moved that night. I prayed with many, some who were drug addicts. One was even ingesting drops of cobra venom, getting "high" on a venom-inspired psychedelic trip. Mark, months later, told me this addict had been saved and was headed to Bible school.

I finished my Calcutta visit and Mark took me to the airport. He said, "Howard, as you fly over India the next ten days, Look down at the villages. There are 600,000 that have never had the gospel." (This trip changed my life forever.) Teen Challenge was planted and is still growing in India, plus the seeds and roots of AIMS targeting unreached people were planted in this Calcutta experience. A fresh vision and new alignment was birthed.

Pause, Reflect, Pray, Plan

1. Are you and your church aligned with obedience to the Great Commission (Matt. 28:19-20, Mark16:15, Luke 24:47, John 17:18; 20:21 and Acts 1:8)?

2. Acts 1:8 contains the last words of Jesus, thus they are weighty and critically important words. Do you pray for targets in Jerusalem, Judea, Samaria, and the ends of the earth?
    How are you aligning your daily actions to these four geographic areas and the unreached peoples they contain?

    _____
    _____
    _____
    _____

3. List two to three alignment and action steps you believe your church should take.

    _____
    _____
    _____
    _____

5

POWER SHIFT #4—ABUNDANCE

Many years ago, that groundbreaking missionary to China, J. Hudson Taylor, explained, "God's work done in God's way will never lack God's supplies."[1] Most of us who live and work in the Great Commission community would utter a hearty "Amen" to that statement, yet it seems like all of us see shortfalls on a regular basis. The hours we spend fundraising should cause us all to re-examine our situations and ask ourselves, "What's wrong with this picture?" Taylor's statement implies that, though we may be doing God's work, we may not be doing it His way.

The biblical books of Exodus through the beginning of Joshua describe Israel's wandering in the wilderness and God's provision for every possible contingency. He led them with a cloud and a fire. He kept their clothes from wearing out. He brought forth water in the desert. And, of course, He fed them with manna. But Joshua 5:12 tells us,

> *"The manna stopped the day after they ate this food from the land; there was no longer any manna for the Israelites, but that year they ate of the produce of Canaan."*

You see, manna was their provision in the wilderness, but the produce of Canaan was their possession in the land God had promised them.

Dominion Based on Servanthood

Joshua 5 gives a clear picture of Israel going in to possess the land of Canaan. It begins with a visit from a heavily armed man who calls himself, at least in one translation, "General-of-the-Army-of-Jehovah." As one commentator notes,

> *God manifested his presence with Israel not as a mere ally but as their leader. It was his war... and the Israelites were only a division of his great army, along with his angels (Ps. 148:2) and the forces of nature (Jos. 10:11-14; Jgs. 5:20). Thus, Joshua immediately perceived he was but the Captain's servant. The account of the conquest makes clear that Joshua's military strategy was divinely directed.*[2]

That strategy, with the eventual goal of taking the whole land, started with one city—Jericho. Defeating Jericho and Ai in the center of Canaan would secure the passes for traveling. It would also divide the northern and southern portions of the region, so the Israelites could go on and conquer the Amorite coalition in the south and the confederacy of nations in the north.

God gave Joshua a specific strategy for the city of Jericho, and He gave them all the resources they needed to accomplish it. It may have seemed like a foolish plan on the surface, to march around the city quietly for six days, then march around seven times on the seventh day, and finally break the silence by blowing horns and shouting. Jericho, after all, was a tremendously strong, walled city. Some historians believe it was the most strongly fortified city in all of Canaan. Yet when the Israelites obediently followed the strategy God gave, acting in His power and in the strength of His provision, the walls of Jericho fell.

The interesting thing, though, is that, while God didn't ask them to replicate that strategy for other cities, He did require absolute obedience to the strategy He gave for each specific situation. And the eventual goal was possession of the entire land (see Joshua 1:3–11). In the Hebrew, the word *Yarash* that we have translated "possess" (or take possession in the NIV) means to "seize, dispossess, occupy, be an heir, take possession of."[3]

The land of Canaan, after all, was already promised to the Israelites in the Abrahamic Covenant (see Genesis 15:16-21).[4] With that understanding, **Alfred Edersheim**, that great **biblical scholar of the nineteenth century,** notes

> **a deeper symbolical meaning attached to the fall of Jericho ... the blast of those jubilee-horns all around the doomed city made proclamation of Jehovah, and was, so to speak, the summons of His kingdom, proclaiming that ... *they were about to enter upon their inheritance* (italics added).[5]**

We need to develop that same mentality today. We need to understand that we are called to possess the nations—that is, the people groups of the world—on behalf of the Lord Jesus Christ. And they've already been given to us. Our ability to experience this power shift toward abundance rests largely on our moving away from a manna mentality (relying on God to give me what I need for today) and moving toward this attitude of dominion. In other words, this new dimension of abundance means trusting God to give me more than enough for myself along with the responsibility to share this abundance with others. We must accept the challenge of our inheritance of "possessing the land."

We need to develop that same mentality today. You see, God gave His Son a promise when He said,

> **Ask of me, and I will make the nations your inheritance, the ends of the earth your possession (Ps. 2:8).**

God challenges us to enlist in the battle to win in practicality what He has already given to His Son positionally.

Our ability to accomplish this rests largely on moving away from a manna mentality and moving toward this attitude of possession. It means trusting God for the resources and the strategy to accomplish this great task. But with the same faith exhibited by the Israelites when they entered Canaan, we must also learn to expect Him to raise up some of those resources from among the peoples we are called to possess.

We see an example of this in South Korea. When Christian missionaries first arrived in that nation, there were no Christians. Now about 30 percent of the population is Christian, and the South Korean church is raising up funding and sending missionaries worldwide.[6] We must adopt this same approach if we are truly serious about finishing the Great Commission. We must exhibit an attitude that leads to possession. Some would call it a dominion mentality.

But I'm suggesting that we develop a dominion mentality based on servanthood. We should not attempt to possess regions and peoples for our own benefit. Rather, we are called to release them from Satan's dominion and place them under God's sovereignty. As Edersheim also reminds us, "The advent of the kingdom of God always implies destruction to His enemies."[7]

For Joshua and the tribes of Israel, that meant it was their job to do battle according to God's revealed plan. God guaranteed the end result, if they were willing to obey. For us, it means the same thing. For instance, it means that, because of the work of Christ on Calvary, the nation of Bhutan is ours. Jesus died for all the Bhutanese. But now He wants you and me, His Church, to seize Bhutan, and every other nation on the face of the earth, and to possess them for His glory through prayer and cooperative outreach so they can hear what God has done for them.

How Is God's Abundance Applied to Missions?

When we learn to accept dominion mentality, and we obediently step out to claim our inheritance, we will find that, when God shuts off the manna, He always enables us to eat the produce of the land.

Within that framework, God's concept of abundance compels us to pass along what God has given us. It requires us to help the next individual, the next locale, the next people group. God's abundance is varied. It comes in multiple kinds of resources, each of which has multiple spinoff benefits.

I believe that concept reveals itself in the contemporary world of missions in six specific ways.

1. Each One Teach Another

First, **we must move from giving fish, and even from teaching people how to fish, to teaching them how to teach their brothers to fish.** We've all heard that giving people fish to eat offers only short-term gains. Teaching people to fish, on the other hand, will enable them to feed themselves for a long time. I suggest that we need to move a step further. We need to train the people so they can teach those who will become fishermen. This is a multiplication principle.

Here's one example: Dr. Solomon Aryeetey of Ghana explains,

No other segment of the body of Christ is better poised to effect a rapid, thorough evangelization of Africa than the African Church itself. With some countries closed to Western missionaries, it makes sense to devise a strategy that will empower the African Church to slip its undercover missionaries into this region.

But, he admits, the African Church lacks resources for the kind of sustained effort required. This is true not only in Africa but many other areas of the world as well.

Is he asking simply for money? No. He says,

African Christians are asking for Western mentors who are willing to "move away from paternalism and toward partnership." They are asking for a comprehensive plan that will transform the dynamic, but poor, African Church into a powerful missionary force. They want to be taught how to raise funds, how to 'make tents' to support themselves, how to handle finances, keep records, and so on.[8]

It is crucial that we hear their request and respond to it. Churches from poorer countries can be used of the Holy Spirit in the gift of mountain-moving faith (1 Cor. 12:9) just as often as western churches. We must empower nationals and help them to be completely self-sufficient in ministry. The multiplication of resources will be incredible.

2. Changed Lives: Spiritual and Social

E. Stanley Jones: "An individual gospel without a social gospel is a soul without a body and a social gospel without an individual gospel is a body without a soul. One is a ghost and the other is a corpse."

We must move from the gospel of Salvation only to the gospel of the Kingdom. We need to accept the fact that God created the whole person, and He is intricately interested in the whole person. His salvation is intended to impact the individual's spirit, but also his mind and body. As **E. Stanley Jones** reminded us, **"An individual gospel without a social gospel is a soul without a body and a social gospel without an individual gospel is a body without a soul. One is a ghost and the other is a corpse."**[9]

Yet, for many years, evangelical missionaries refused these concepts. Many serving in South America, for instance, would not involve themselves in social ministry at all. They stressed only the individual gospel, ministering to the spirit but ignoring physical needs. In Jones' words, they built a corpse. Out of that context, the foundation was set for their misdirected missions strategy and was partly responsible for the birth of Liberation Theology. And in the beginning, it held some truth. Now, Liberation Theology redefines sin and salvation, pushing men and women to "fight oppression" even through revolution, Liberation Theology stands in the way of true freedom—the liberty Christ offers which defies logic, for it cannot be limited by any earthly means.

We must learn a strategic lesson from the failures we have seen at both ends of the spectrum. **The bottom line here is that the Church of Jesus Christ must be involved in social ministry, but that ministry must have evangelistic direction.** I remember reading several articles in major newspapers detailing the results of Assemblies of God missions activity in Brazil. One noted, "It appears that Protestant converts in Latin America are less likely to steal, drink, beat their wives or abandon their children. The second generation is already moving quickly into the professions."[10]

You see, when the gospel shows up and changes people's lives, even the secular press notices. Those newspapers described communities where the gospel had penetrated, and the people reaped social and economic rewards as a result. Why? They quit buying alcohol, tobacco, and drugs and paying for prostitutes. They quit gambling away their salaries and started buying groceries and investing in homes. They began helping one another, bearing one another's burdens, as Scripture requires. The gospel didn't just penetrate their spirits—it changed their lives. And it changed them so drastically that secular newspapers, headquartered thousands of miles away, took notice.

If we are truly going to impact the world in which we live, we must strive for those kinds of results. We must not settle for what E. Stanley Jones called the ghost or the corpse. We must minister to the whole man—spirit, mind, and body—knowing that the God Who created man in His image is interested in every part of His creation.

3. Strategize for Closure

We must move from "plan-so-far" strategies to unique strategies that lead to closure. As I define it, a "plan-so-far" strategy is one that says, "This is how we've done it so far..."[12] It's a misguided effort that may be rooted in the best of intentions, but it isn't necessarily focused on the end vision of building God's Kingdom.

Isaiah records several revelations from the Lord, and two of them reveal an interesting juxtaposition of words that relate very well to this issue. Isaiah 46:9 has God saying,

> *Remember the former things, those of long ago; I am God, and there is no other; I am God, and there is none like me.*

But just a few brief pages before that, Isaiah 43:18–19a has God saying,

Forget the former things; do not dwell on the past. See, I am doing a new thing!

So how can we remember and forget at the same time? The answer, of course, lies in the words that follow those two phrases. We are to remember God's character as it has been revealed in the past:

Remember the former things, those of long ago; I am God, and there is no other; I am God, and there is none like me. I make known the end from the beginning, from ancient times, what is still to come. I say, "My purpose will stand, and I will do all that I please." (Isaiah 46:9)

But relative to our current situations, we are to forget—that is, we are not to expect God to only repeat His past patterns of accomplishing things. He's too big and too creative to accept the limitations of our traditions:

Forget the former things; do not dwell on the past. (Isaiah 43:18)

Unfortunately, a lot of missions effort is based on a general mix-up of our remembering and forgetting. Instead of viewing history with an idea of seeing the revelation of God's character, we use past experience to build structures and strategies that, if He allowed it, would stifle His ability to act in a different way. In the missions community, that amounts to little progress toward completing the Great Commission.

I believe that every missions strategy must answer one serious question: How will this help the effort to take the gospel of the Kingdom to every people group in the world?

Please understand that I'm not suggesting you cut off resources immediately to all missionaries who aren't specifically involved in working toward closure. If you're supporting general missionaries working in areas that are already heavily evangelized, don't call them back, and don't stop supporting them while they're on the field. Instead, when they come home for furlough, why don't you try to re-educate them and envision them for the unreached? If they're working in Brazil or Mexico or Jamaica, places that have strong churches that are capable of evangelizing their own people and even of sending missionaries elsewhere, try to help your missionary become more strategic. Help them find specialized niches where they can extend what the national church is able to do on its own, or where they can train people to fulfill a new avenue of ministry. One thing they can always do is to mobilize the national church and train it to send out its own missionaries.

Working toward closure—the completion of the Great Commission —that must be the overarching goal of every investment of time, personnel, money, or other resources.

4. Establish Church-Planting Movements

We must move from planting single churches to establishing church-planting movements. This flows naturally out of the previous point, and since I have covered it elsewhere in the book, I won't spend a lot of time on it now. It will suffice to note that this particular change in strategy alone would greatly accelerate the rate at which we are moving toward closure.

I visited one such church in India, which is now one of the largest churches in its entire nation. I know a missionary friend who raised mega dollars to build this great church, which now has planted forty additional churches in its own city and is sending out missionaries cross-culturally throughout the nation of India. This is a fountainhead church that will trigger a movement.

We must establish churches like this one that have a healthy interest in reproduction. We must invest in churches and church-planting movements that are able to evangelize their own people groups to the fringes, and that will also raise up missionaries who are willing to minister in a cross-cultural framework.

5. Giving Motivated by Obedience and Biblical Stewardship

We must move from an attitude of "raising money" to the stewardship of God's blessings. This has at least two positive results. First, it provides for long-term ministry rather than forcing churches and mission agencies to consistently raise money on a project-by-project basis. Second, it releases us from a consumer marketing mentality.

I have one friend who founded a missionary organization to reach unreached people groups. He ended up doing primarily social ministry. Why? His reason, because that's what raises money. We cannot afford to allow ourselves to be limited by that kind of mentality. We must teach churches to give because of obedience and through biblical stewardship. God has abundant resources. None of us will deny that. If we will steward effectively what He gives, and learn to give in increasing abundance, we will have all the resources we need to complete the Great Commission.

And the good news is, God will never allow His local churches to suffer for giving on behalf of those who still wait for the gospel. Time after time in my association with local churches, I have found that God has honored those who have shown compassion for the lost through their giving. Pastors have told me repeatedly of financial miracles that their congregations experienced only after they committed to missions giving. We don't ever have to be afraid to obey His mandate.

6. Abundance: Divine River of Resources

We must move from a pie mentality to a river mentality. The pie mentality says every department gets its "slice of the budgetary pie." This leads to competition as the different departments strive to gain more money for future "ministry." God never plops a pie down in front of us and says, "Okay, y'all. Divvy it up now." Instead, He gives us a river of blessings in our relationship with Him. And part of His covenant is the creation of wealth. Scripture clearly tells us, "But remember the LORD your God, for it is he who gives you the ability to produce wealth, and so confirms his covenant, which he swore to your forefathers, as it is today" (Deut. 8:18).

God's resources are like a river rather than a pie—they can deepen and widen as the need arises. When we begin to experience this, we will find that "Deep and Wide" is more than just a Sunday school song—it's a way of life. If we willingly bless others as God has blessed us, He will more than meet us halfway in providing for ministry.

> God's resources are like a river rather than a pie—they can deepen and widen as the need arises.

Our Lady's Youth Center in El Paso, Texas, is a perfect example. Under the leadership of Father Rick Thomas, in the early 1970s, a prayer group at the youth center read in Luke 14:12-14, "When you give a dinner or a banquet, do not invite your friends or your brothers." They decided to take this passage literally, and they believed "God was calling them to celebrate Christmas dinner with the residents of the garbage dump in Juarez, Mexico. They went to the dump, negotiated a truce between the dump's factions, and served the dinner. Only later did they realize that they had served twice the number of dinners than they had brought."[13]

Our God is not poor. He owns it all—the cattle on a thousand hills, as Scripture tells us. And He's willing to provide for us. The same God who met the Juarez dump people's needs and J. Hudson Taylor's needs will meet ours with an abundant river of resources.

But we must remember—God's resources are not to be hoarded. Still water grows stagnant. A river stays fresh because it continues to flow, taking the water to others who live further downstream.

A Glimpse of a Strategic Power Shift in Abundance

My pastor, Dr. Charles Blair, and I made our way out of Addis Ababa, Ethiopia, to Debre Zeit where the main orphanage of Kale Hiwot was located, the largest denomination in Ethiopia. Girma Abebe, director of the orphanage, adjusted the sleeping quarters of the children so we (AIMS) could have our first training for pastors. Seven hundred from seventeen denominations came. They responded enthusiastically to reaching the (then sixty) unreached people groups in Ethiopia. I was deeply impressed with the high quality of leadership in Ethiopia, but I was surprised that no denomination had a single indigenous missionary. This first training stimulated thirty-seven more trainings in the following thirty years.

Girma Abebe became one of my closest friends, and he was asked to start a missions department for his denomination. Ethiopia became a model country in applying our AIMS training in missions mobilization and church planting. Through our training in faith promise giving, they began raising up indigenous missionaries and sent them to unreached peoples. Now they have over twelve hundred missionaries, have planted hundreds of churches, and are now sending missionaries to neighboring countries and even as far as China.

Ethiopia is not an economically rich country, but the believers and churches are rich in faith and obedience. They have learned not to be totally dependent on outside resources, they have moved away from the "pie mentality" to the "river mentality." This demonstrates a significant power shift to abundance and dominion. And, it's not only Kale Hiwot, for the denominations involved in our training ministry have reduced the number of unreached people groups from over sixty to thirty-five.

Pause, Reflect, Pray, Plan

1.   How are you and your church doing in training everyone in biblical stewardship? Is the giving strategic?

2.   List two to three ways you could increase your gift of faith and the application of the "river, not pie," mentality.

_____

_____

_____

_____

3. List two to three ways you and your church could use the teaching of this chapter to generate more giving to missions.

    _____

    _____

    _____

    _____

6

POWER SHIFT # 5—ANOINTING

I heard of a young lady who thought one specific Bible was the only one you should read. Please understand, I'm not talking about the raging debate over which version of the Bible is acceptable—I mean there was one Bible with specific commentary that she thought was "anointed." She claimed this because she thought it was written on the Bible's binding—"Dr. So-and-So's Anointed Bible." She was, of course, misreading the word "annotated."

That young woman's mistake gives cause for a brief chuckle, but it also tellingly illustrates the misunderstanding that swirls around the concept of anointing. The anointing of God is illustrated throughout the Bible and missions history. Without the anointing of God, life and ministry is shallow, without depth and lacking in fruit.

The Biblical Pattern

Scripture gives many examples of anointing, for it was a common practice in the culture of the Middle Eastern region. We know, for instance, that rubbing oil on the hair and body was considered part of the general process of getting dressed—like some people rub lotion on their bodies now (see Ruth 3:3). The use of oil or ointment was considered an expression of joy and celebration (see Ps. 23:5), and the lack of it indicated grief or sadness (see 2 Sam. 14:2, Dan. 10:3). We also know it was considered an act of hospitality to anoint a guest (Luke 7:46), and that oils and ointments were sometimes used medicinally (see Isa. 1:6, Mark 6:13).[1]

However, the Bible also demonstrates that, in some cases, anointing had a special, spiritual connotation. It represented something or someone being set apart, or consecrated, and empowered for God's service. We know, for instance, that God required anointing for those people who were to assume three specific offices among His people.

The Anointed Kings

Historically, the Israelites had lived without a king. After Moses, they were led by Joshua, and then by a series of judges whom God raised up and empowered to deliver them in times of trouble. However, as the judge and prophet Samuel neared the end of his career, somewhere around 1000 BC, the people, influenced by their environment and wanting to be like their neighbors, requested a king. After debating with the people and interceding on their behalf before God, Samuel finally agreed, and God told him to anoint Saul (see 1 Sam. 9:16). That initiated the tradition of a monarchy and the anointing of kings, who represented dominion and authority, and who were positioned by God to carry out specific tasks, especially in leading the Israelites into war and in executing judgment and justice.

The Anointed Priests

Priests are necessary because of sin. Underlying the concept of the priesthood is the understanding that sin separates us from God, so that we need a mediator. Before the Israelites went into bondage in Egypt and during their captivity, fathers served as priests for their families. Then, in their wilderness experience after leaving Egypt, God's preparation to make them a nation included raising up one specific family (Aaron's) and consecrating its members to serve as priests.

Aaron's anointing represents this change from the father being the family's priest to the family of Aaron becoming the nation's priests (see

Ex. 28:41). His family assumed the responsibility to go to God on behalf of a sinful people. But in order to take on that challenge, each participating priest had to go through the ceremony of anointing described in Exodus 29:1-34.

The Anointed Prophets

Like a priest, a prophet is a mediator. The difference, though, is that a priest goes to God on behalf of the people, but the prophet comes to the people on behalf of God. A prophet is "one who is divinely inspired to communicate God's will to his people and to disclose the future to them." In Scripture, he admonished the people and reproved them for their sin; he brought warnings of terrible judgment, but he also brought the message of consolation and pardon. And sometimes, he performed miracles. First and Second Kings are full of the supernatural events that surrounded the ministries of Elijah and Elisha, for instance. The power of God was activated in the prophet's life through consecration, and that consecration was symbolized by anointing (see I Kgs. 19:16 for an example).[2]

The Anointed One: Spiritually Empowered

The Hebrew language uses the word *mashach* to describe the anointing that consecrated the men who assumed all three of those offices. That word simply means "to rub with oil." The Septuagint, a Greek translation of the Old Testament, uses the word *chrio*, which is the root word for the name Christ, which literally means "The Anointed One." In this context, it's easy to understand that a physical anointing represents God pouring out the Holy Spirit on someone to empower him or her to accomplish the task to which God has called that individual.[3]

Jesus' friends and neighbors who were sitting in the synagogue at Nazareth would have understood all of this when, on a return visit home, Jesus had the honor of reading the Scripture passage for the day. Turning to an Old Testament prophetic passage (Isaiah 61), Jesus noted, "The Spirit of the Lord is on me, because he has anointed me...." He then told the people in attendance, "Today this scripture is fulfilled in your hearing." This was basically a proclamation of His position as the long-awaited Messiah. Jesus began his anointed ministry preaching the kingdom of God, and this proved that the Father had sent him.

When they hesitated because, after all, they had seen Him grow up and <u>were</u> sure He was "just a man," Jesus went on to tell them that He knew they would not accept Him. And, He reminded them, that same attitude demonstrated by others throughout Hebrew history had often limited God's ability to work in the midst of His chosen people, even while He was free to accomplish great things among people of other nations (see Luke 4:14-27).

The bottom line here is that Jesus, as God's Anointed One, fulfilled all three offices that were crucial to the life of the nation of Israel: King, Priest, and Prophet.

He was (and is) **the King** of the entire world.

Ask of me," God told His Son, "and I will make the nations your inheritance, the ends of the earth your possession. (Psalm 2:7-8)

He owns it all, and He rules it all.

He was (and is) **the Priest** for all mankind, serving as the mediator between God and man. We who have accepted His sacrifice on our behalf have the right to enter God's presence, and

for this reason Christ is the mediator of a new covenant, that those who are called may receive the promised eternal inheritance. (Heb. 9:15).

Finally, He was (and is) **the Prophet**—God's spokesperson. His announcement to the people of Nazareth begins and ends with His call to

"preach the good news to the poor" and to "proclaim the year of the Lord's favor."

Those two items, preach and proclaim, sandwiched His description of a ministry of miracles, which would enable Him

to proclaim freedom for the prisoners and recovery of sight to the blind, to release the oppressed (Isa. 61:1–2, Luke 4:18–19).

Truly, Jesus Christ was and is the complete package—King, Priest, and Prophet.

Christians: "Little Anointed Ones"

Most of us would agree, I think, that a "Christian" is one who follows Christ—one who imitates His character and His actions. Scripture tells us Jesus' followers were first called Christians in Antioch (see Acts 11:26). But the English translation doesn't really clarify what that word literally means. The residents of the city of Antioch were literally calling these neophyte believers "little Christs."

In the context of this discussion, then, let me point out that a "little Christ" is actually a "little anointed one." Being a Christian involves much more than just escaping the eternal torture of judgment in hell. Scripture reminds us that we are saved by faith, completely by God's grace, but also that "we are God's workmanship, created in Christ Jesus to do good works, which God prepared in advance for us to do" (Eph. 2:8-10). Our actions don't save us, but they do reflect the change in character that occurs as we imitate Christ.

It only makes sense, then, that **the "works" we do as individuals and as local churches and as the Church should be the same as the works Christ did.** *We are empowered to serve as kings,* under His ultimate headship, leading God's people into spiritual warfare and assuming authority over everything that would seek to hinder our success (see Luke 10:19-20). *We are empowered to serve as priests,* seeking God's mercy on behalf of a sinful

> The "works" we do as individuals and as local churches and as the Church should be the same as the works Christ did.

and dying world (see 1 Pet. 2:9). And *we are empowered to serve as prophets*, giving God's message of love and discipline, and expecting His Spirit to work through us to accomplish those things that cannot be rationally explained (see Acts 1:8, 2:17-21).

God's Power Demonstrated in Global Evangelization

The western church, unfortunately, has a history of trying to do God's work in our own strength. Globally, we have accomplished some pretty useful things. We have educated indigenous populations. We have built and staffed hospitals. We have preached revivals and evangelized many parts of the world. Yet for the most part, because our worldview was so broadly affected by the rationalism that demands sensory evidence, we have ignored the reality of the spiritual world. As one missionary explained,

> *There is the constant invisible warfare that has to be waged against the powers of darkness. It is fashionable in the Western world to relegate belief in demons and devils to the realm of mythology, and when mentioned at all, it is a matter of jest. But it is no jest in West Africa or any other mission field for that matter.*[4]

If we intend to win the war that he spoke of, we must be sensitive to cultural practices and worldviews. We must have the empowerment of the Holy Spirit if we are to win these souls to the Lord. I believe these simple facts must be lived out in the missions community in four specific ways.

1. Spirituality: A Lens for Viewing All of Life

We must move from doing missions according to a secular Western mentality to understanding the spiritual framework within which indigenous cultures live. The Western worldview divides life into exclusively spiritual and secular categories, and it has established specific institutions to deal with each category. We go to church for the spiritual, to the doctor for the physical, to school for the intellectual, and to our court system for the judicial. In this mindset, the categories don't meet very often. The non-Western mindset is quite different.

F. Kefa Sempangi founded and pastored a 14,000-member church in Uganda. His position made him a target of persecution under the regime of Idi Amin. He later reflected on his experiences in a book called *A Distant Grief*. Sempangi explained, **"'Truth' for a non-westernized African does not refer to a statement's correspondence with a fact. Truth is a quality of things. A mango tree is true if it bears sweet mangoes, a house is true if it is up-right."** Within that context,

> "'Truth' for a non-westernized African does not refer to a statement's correspondence with a fact. Truth is a quality of things. A mango tree is true if it bears sweet mangoes, a house is true if it is up-right."

A religion is true if it works, if it meets all the needs of the people. *A religion that speaks only to man's soul and not to his body is not true. Africans make no distinction between the spiritual and the physical. The spiritual is not a category among categories but the lens through which all of life is viewed. A tribesman from my village knows that cutting a tree, climbing a mountain, making a fire, planting a garden, and bowing before the gods are all religious acts. He lives in the presence of the gods, and he knows that without intervention from them there is nothing. There is no coffee harvest, no wood for the fire, no wife, no children.*

Sempangi told of two individuals who came to him separately with specific problems, and they both told him that if God couldn't help, they knew their traditional gods and goddesses could. He concluded, "At the time I found these remarks offensive, but now I understood that both people had one thing in common: They were not looking for a worldview but for a power to transform their lives. If Christianity could not help them, the witch doctor could."[5]

According to Marguerite Kraft, who completed lengthy studies of three different indigenous cultures, non-Western people who have a holistic worldview tend to meet "felt needs" with spiritual resources. Those needs basically fall into six categories: 1) perpetuity needs—primarily concerned with maintaining lineage, tribe, and people; 2) prosperity needs; 3) health needs; 4) security needs—often required in times of natural disaster; 5) restitution needs—for instance, when spirits have been offended and must be appeased; 6) power needs—desiring to gain control over things that are unknown or not understood.[6]

This is the realm in which missionaries work when they minister to cultures outside the Western world. Indeed, as New Age philosophies and other religions invade our own "developed" nations, it is increasingly the realm in which we work in the West as well. We are called to serve a world full of needy people who think they have to manipulate and trick "the powers that be" into performing on their behalf. They won't accept pat doctrinal answers—they want real answers to real problems, and we can only provide that in the power of the Holy Spirit.

2. God's Power Stronger Than All Spirit Powers

We must move from ignoring spirit powers to emphasizing God's omnipotence over all spirit powers. Elijah, who ministered in a culture not unlike today's non-Western societies, accomplished this attitude when he met the prophets of Baal on Mt. Carmel (see I Kings 18:18-46). Baal was a weather god, and the Israelites succumbed to the idea that they had to appease him in order to have a bountiful harvest. To paraphrase a contemporary saying, they thought, *If Baal ain't happy, ain't nobody happy.*

In the Scriptural record of Elijah's confrontation with Baal's followers, we see no hint that he sought to convince them that their god didn't exist. He simply demonstrated the supremacy of the Lord God Almighty over Baal. The Lord met the people in the territory of their idol. Elijah declared God was going to dry up the sky, and no rain would fall for a certain period. It happened, just as Elijah said it would, and then God took Elijah to Mt.

Carmel to confront the religious leaders and the people who followed this false god.

You probably remember the resulting contest. Baal's prophets built an altar and prayed for their god to burn up the sacrifice they placed there. After several hours, Elijah actually began to taunt them. "Shout louder!" he said. "Surely he is a god! Perhaps he is deep in thought, or busy, or traveling. Maybe he is sleeping and must be awakened." Elijah let those false priests exhaust themselves, and then he took his turn. He built an altar to the Lord. He put the sacrifice on it and soaked the whole thing with water. Then he prayed, and within a few seconds, the sacrifice, the altar, the water, even the dust that surrounded it, had disappeared in the fire that fell from God in heaven.

Elijah, representing the true God of all gods, demonstrated His omnipotence over all menial regional spiritual powers that would attempt to stand in the way of accomplishing His purposes.

Now, some would say that kind of event can't happen in the present day. But here's an example: Kouton Pierre, a Baptist convert living in Benin, West Africa, grew up under the influence of a fetish cult headed by his mother. However, his survival of a bout with pneumonia convinced him of Christ's superiority. Kouton Pierre worked as a rural development agent, and about six months after his conversion, his government sent him to a village near the Togo border. There he developed a work among the Ife people. He shared his knowledge of rural development, but also shared his newfound faith.

One day a thunderstorm delayed Pierre from coming home, and when he finally arrived, he found that his house had been hit by lightning and was now surrounded by people, several of whom were fetish leaders. Neighbors called the local religious leaders of which Pierre was a part, to make a sacrifice to the lightning god. When he refused, everyone thought he would be immediately struck by lightning and die. When this didn't happen, the villagers believed God was stronger than their lightning god.

People began inviting him into their homes and asked him to tell them about Jesus. Visitors from neighboring villages also began to come as well. As a result, people were converted and now churches are being planted throughout the area.[7] Kouton simply trusted in God's omnipotence over all spirit powers. He withstood the pressure to conform to the demands of a false god, and in the process, he ascribed glory to the one true God. He allowed God to demonstrate His power.

3. Power Encounters Demonstrate the Gospel

We must move from just teaching the gospel to demonstrating the gospel. An AIMS staff member recently returned from a reunion of missionaries, most of whom served in what is now the Democratic Republic of Congo in the 1940s through the 1980s. As she was waiting for one of the meetings to begin, she overheard the tail end of a conversation occurring in the row behind her. "You know," one of the speakers said, "we worked hard when we were in the Congo. But we didn't do anything about the witchcraft, and we didn't pray for people for supernatural healing. I think we missed the boat." This was a revelation, a bit late in coming, but an important truth.

> "Missions is not applied anthropology, comparative religion, and sociology. It is storming the gates of hell. It is a power confrontation—hand-to-hand combat with Satan and his demons."

The simple fact is, if we are truly going to make any kind of lasting difference in the lives of millions of people worldwide, we must demonstrate the power of the gospel. One national missionary leader has noted, "This kind of authoritative witness is essential on most mission fields, lands where evil manifestations of demon power are routine. Billions of people are still held captive to idol and spirit worship, beginning and ending their days with ritual offerings. They burn incense and sacrifice the living to satiate horrible spirits that animate their idols for millions of people enslaved in spiritual darkness; they must see evidence of something better and stronger than their idol gods and shrines." This author adds, **"Missions is not applied anthropology, comparative religion, and sociology. It is storming the gates of hell. It is a power confrontation—**

hand-to-hand combat with Satan and his demons."[8]

Missionary anthropologist Alan Tippett coined a term for that kind of confrontation between the Kingdom of God and the Kingdom of Darkness. In his classic *People Movements in Southern Polynesia,* Tippett wrote of a Christian chief who received a turtle as a gift. In his culture, that turtle was to be held sacred and was to be offered to an idol. Instead, this chief had it cooked, and then he publicly ate it. His frightened people refused to eat with him, and they were amazed when nothing happened to him. He had successfully demonstrated that his God was more powerful than any local deity.

Tippett called that kind of event a "power encounter." He later explained, "In presenting the gospel, the missionary advocated a plan of salvation. Many of his hearers needed no convincing of this, for sin and fear were real. They understood the need of salvation. They did not doubt the power of the God about whom the missionaries spoke." However, he added, "The superiority of that salvation had to be proved by practical demonstration. Somewhere there had to be an actual encounter between Christ and the old god."[9]

Tippett's term "power encounter" has since expanded to include other events that cannot be explained rationally—ministry events like supernatural healing and deliverance from demonic forces. All of these events demonstrate the supremacy of our God over all other spiritual forces.

Many Western Christians have accepted the reality of Satan's existence and know that he seeks to engage the followers of Christ in battle. Still, our response has frequently tended to be theoretical rather than practical. The limitations of that response are becoming increasingly evident, both among other cultures and within our own.

As one author noted, "Missionaries who avoid, or even deny, the demonic in daily life create a perplexing problem for the indigenous churches. On the one hand, they teach how Jesus cast out demons, but on the other they refuse to incorporate the problem of demonization within the scope of the church's ministry." The result of that kind of dichotomy is an integration of Christianity and local religions, also known as syncretism.

The nationals learn to "look to the church for the forgiveness of sin and eternal life but go to the shaman or diviner to receive solutions to problems that the church, or the missionary, cannot answer. Unfortunately, they think that Jesus and the church are impotent in the very area where he (Jesus) exercises supreme authority and dominion."[10]

To illustrate this point, let me offer another story from Kefa Sempangi, who tells of a time that some people from his congregation brought a woman on a stretcher to him. She had seen her husband brutally murdered. She herself had been raped and severely beaten by Idi Amin's soldiers. Her house had been plundered, and in her despair, she attempted to commit suicide. Having failed in this suicide attempt, she was found and brought to Sempangi.

Sempangi grew angry with the group and told them to take the woman to the hospital. "We are not doctors here," he said. "We are preachers of the Word."

There was complete silence until an elderly woman standing quietly in the background suddenly spoke up. She too was angry but for entirely different reasons. She addressed Sempangi with an uncompromising voice as she gathered herself up stiffly in indignation. "Do you think," she said, 'that when people brought their sick friends to Jesus, they didn't know where the hospital was?"[11]

That question poses a haunting question for all of us, but perhaps especially for those who serve on the mission field, because we preach against the people who seem to have a demonically inspired answer to the perplexities of life suffered as evidenced in the poverty and demon-laden world in which most of the world's population find themselves. Sempangi's resulting vigil with this woman, her eventual healing, and the salvation of her family and of many others, only came because he was confronted with a profound and currently relevant truth. Sempangi has since asked, "What business do we have destroying the people's doctors if we don't know what to do with their sick?"[12]

What business have we, indeed? However, we should also note that relying solely on the power encounter for ministry will not build a strong indigenous church of healthy believers. Charles Kraft notes, "These people are accustomed to accepting power from any source. Therefore, they see no greater compulsion to commit themselves to Jesus than to any of the other sources of power they regularly consult."

Of course, this shouldn't take us by surprise. Many people who witnessed or even experienced healing and deliverance under Christ's ministry did not commit their lives to following Him. Kraft writes, "This should alert us to the inadequacy of power demonstrations alone as a total evangelistic strategy." Within that framework, then, we must remember to give adequate attention to the truth of Scripture, which teaches God's character and His expectations for those who follow Him, and to individual witness, which calls people to commitment and to a personal relationship with Christ. The three must be bound together: power, teaching, and personal witness. In that framework, we will see true, long-lasting growth among individuals and among churches.[13]

4. Prepare Western Churches for Power Encounters

We must move from training only our missionaries for power encounters to training our Western congregations for them. The simple truth is that missionaries of all denominations are seeing power encounters on the field. God is responding to the needs of millions of people who have lived in Satan's grasp for far too long. He is pouring out His Holy Spirit to empower His representatives, and they are confronting Satan in his own territory, with incredible results.

However, many Western congregations are still struggling with this power shift. One of our AIMS staff members told me of a missionary who serves in Latin America on behalf of an evangelical denomination. This missionary actually saw a young lady raised to life after being dead for several days. She was excited! She wanted to share it with her friends at home! But when she returned for deputation, her leaders told her not to tell Americans about the event. "They won't believe it," her leaders told her. "They'll think you're crazy." *For a video about Fatima, a former Muslim woman who was raised from the dead, visit www.aims.org.

Instead of muzzling our missionaries, we need to teach this concept to our Western churches. Otherwise, they will miss the blessing of knowing that God, who raises people from the dead, can handle any problem they face. They will never understand the full power of the God they serve. They will never know the divine validation of the ministry they support with their prayers and their finances. And finally, they will be unprepared to truly minister in a Western world that is increasingly bowing to the demon-laden religions that have kept millions of people in physical, mental, emotional, and spiritual bondage for centuries. Truly, God will hold us accountable if we refuse to confront our Western churches with the reality of His power.

A Glimpse of a Strategic Power Shift in Anointing

It is an extraordinary blessing for me and all our AIMS trainers to work with outstanding indigenous pastors and leaders around the world. Our calling is to envision, train, and network churches together to initiate church planting movements in targeted unreached people groups. We certainly are not against sending more Western missionaries, but in many situations, national, indigenous workers are the most culturally orientated and therefore the best messengers. So our focus is partnering with national churches, training them to raise up and support their own missionaries to plant churches where there have been none. This puts the responsibility where it ultimately belongs—with a mature fully functioning indigenous church. Western missionaries are vitally needed in training, specialized ministry like business as missions and technology, strategic networking, and humanitarian ministries.

With humility and thankfulness to God for his guidance and anointing, I share the following results of our training partnership with national movements. This is God's testimony! The statistics from October 1995 to August 2018 are:

- Pastors and Leaders Trained: 171,875
- Churches Planted by Partners: 54,444

- Gospel Presentations: 34,849,850
- Salvations: 3,247,887

I see this as a power shift in the AIMS ministry, all for God's glory. Now we are trusting God for another power shift by putting our training on the internet and enabling networking and reporting to be done through computers and smartphones. Please review the "Glimpse of a Strategic Power Shift in Action" on pp 22-23. This is how we intend to engage partners with indigenous workers to adopt and reach thirty-five hundred unreached people groups.

Pause, Reflect, Pray, Plan

1. How is your church doing in Spirit-empowered ministry, deliverance ministry, and power encounters?

2. What are two to three areas around your church that would be ideal for these types of ministry?

   _____

   _____

   _____

   _____

3. List two to three ways your church could bring this kind of anointed ministry into the teaching and practical ministry of your church.

   _____

   _____

   _____

   _____

7

FOR SUCH A TIME AS THIS:
REBELLING AGAINST THE STATUS QUO

This book has challenged the Christian missions community to rebel against the status quo. Our traditional methods have been instrumental in evangelizing half of the world; that is true. But the half that is evangelized is slowly returning to the cults and "isms" that we thought were left behind. And the 40-50 percent that has never been evangelized still waits for the life-changing Gospel of Jesus Christ. The bottom line here is that we must change our method of operations so we don't take another 2,000 years to complete the final task Christ gave His followers before He returned to His Father in Heaven.

That means we must make ourselves available to what God wants to do in this generation. And I believe He wants to give His Church—the Bride of Christ, which He intends to use in His plan to win the world—a new understanding and experience of His power. Throughout this book, we have called that a **power shift**.

However, I don't believe that power shifts occur one at a time. We in the West tend to think in a linear fashion. We believe you start at the beginning and proceed step-by-step until you reach the end. Much of life, and especially life in the Spirit, can't be explained that way. Instead of linear, it's circular. In this context, our attitudes become actions, our actions necessitate alignment, our alignment releases abundant resources, which hopefully will happen in concert with an acceptance of God's anointing. Each power shift gains momentum from and feeds into the others.

It's a little bit like the fruit of the Spirit. Perhaps you've noticed that Paul didn't say the fruits of the Spirit, as if we could take two or three and leave the others for someone else. The fruit of the Spirit is God's character revealed in us. Certainly, it has different expressions, but God expects believers to reflect all of the fruit.

Power shifts are the same way. We can't pick and choose from among them and expect them to have the same effect they have together. And they must be developed in the context of prayer.

This book was written primarily to challenge the Church to reconsider the missions status quo, which has left us with half of the world unevangelized, despite 2,000 years of labor in its harvest fields. Within that context, the comments of David F. Wells take on additional significance. Wells believes prayer is the most basic form of "rebelling against the status quo." **Petitionary prayer, he says,**

> **is, in essence, rebellion—rebellion against the world in its fallenness, the absolute and undying refusal to accept as normal what is pervasively abnormal. It is, in this negative aspect, the refusal of every agenda, every scheme, every interpretation that is at odds with the norm as originally established by God.**[1]

And so I challenge you to rebel against the status quo by prayerfully considering the conclusions on which this book is based. We live in an information-laden society. We have succumbed to the idea that information yields power. But we have lost the true significance of information in the tidal wave of data that has threatened to drown us. You see, information only has power as it changes the way we think and behave. **Petitionary Prayers: its authority lies in its application.**

If you read this book, ponder its conclusions, and then put it on your shelf and promptly forget it, I've accomplished nothing. I challenge you, therefore, to earnestly bring my conclusions to God. Seek His face and ask Him if they are true or untrue. If you come away convinced that they are true, ask Him how He wants you to apply them.

We face a situation like that of the sower in our Lord's parable, which we quoted at the beginning of this book. We can't afford to continue settling for the thirty-fold harvest when God has provided for the hundred-fold yield.

We live in a crucial, strategic age. We must not miss His provision for this generation. That's what utilizing power shifts are all about.

POWER SHIFTS

GLOSSARY OF ENGLISH TERMS
(as used in this book)

Alignment – adjusting our priorities and strategies to line up with God's.

Closure – completion of the Great Commission (sharing salvation through Christ Jesus and making disciples among all people groups throughout the world.)

Cross-cultural ministry – when people from one social, work and belief system attempt to communicate about God in ways that speak to the heart and in the language of peoples with different customs, lifestyles, or language patterns.

Dead-end missions – endeavors which do not indigenize the work by encouraging and training nationals to assume responsibility for the ministry and even to send out their own missionaries.

Dispossess – to deprive someone of possession; seize, occupy, take possession of.

Entrenchment – "missions compound mentality," entrenching into our own culture and not opening ourselves up in vulnerability to our national brothers and sisters and their emerging leaders.

Holistic cooperation – laying aside our differences and choosing to work together for a common purpose. Groups from different languages and cultures, denominations, parachurch organizations, all working together in a coordinated effort with a unified goal to fulfill the Great Commission.

Indigenous cultures – the customary beliefs, social forms, and behavioral codes that govern a group of people in their home or natural environment.

Indigenization – training and mentoring national church workers to assume responsibilities initially carried by foreign missionaries; the withdrawal of foreign manpower as godly native leaders are able to take over the Christian work.

National – a citizen of that country; for example, a citizen of Nigeria is a Nigerian national.

Paradigm – a pattern, outline, theory, or perception; an assumption or frame of reference; a worldview or the "mental filters" through which we interpret reality.

Paradigm shift – a change in our worldview, which, in turn, affects the way we interpret reality.

Power shift – employing prophetic vision, biblical wisdom, and comprehensive understanding and insight to develop a higher level of productivity.

Reactive churches – churches that prefer to remain in the status quo and resist change, especially in long-cherished ideas. This results in faulty and often unbiblical thinking. This kind of church responds to fads rather than proactively responding to God's vision and purpose.

Reformation – the sixteenth-century effort to correct errors in the life and teaching of Christianity in Europe, resulting in the separation of the Protestant churches from the Roman Catholic Church.

Sectarianism - confined to the dogmatic limits of a sect; partisan; characterized by bigoted adherence to a viewpoint that is narrow in scope or divisive.

Strategic churches – churches that hold the goal of reaching the world for Christ in sight while making each decision.

Synergism - the actions of two or more chemicals or organisms working together to achieve an effect which neither was capable of accomplishing alone; spiritually, an explosion of power when entities coordinate their efforts by working together to expand the borders of God's kingdom.

Typology - a way of classifying information in terms of foreshadowing. A recorded person or thing or event is seen as foreshadowing a person or thing or event in the future. For instance, the Passover foreshadowed, or is a "type" of, Christ's sacrificial death to redeem mankind.

POWER SHIFTS

GLOSSARY OF GREEK TERMS
(as used in this book)

Chrio – anoint. This is the Greek equivalent of the Hebrew word *Mashach*, which means to rub with oil. Specifically, for our purposes, it refers to the anointing of individuals to assume one of three offices: prophet, priest, or king.

Christos – a person who has been anointed. This is the Greek equivalent of the Hebrew word Messiah.

Chronos – time measured by calendars and clocks.

Diakanos – a servant in relationship with his work, serving the needs of others.

Doulos – a slave bound to his master so closely that only death can break the yoke.

Ethne – peoples; in missions, people groups sharing the same ethnicity, culture, and language.

Exousia – delegated authority given for a specific purpose, as Jesus' authority was to do the will of the Father.

Huperetes – under-oarsman, one who takes the hardest and least-honored work.

Kairos - the moment of opportunity. A "Kairos moment" is when God sets all details in order and opens the door for people to go along with God in what He's about to accomplish.

Koinonia - communion, fellowship, sharing. Different forms of this word also imply partnership in a task.

Sophos Architekton – expert builder; one who knows his profession and applies wisdom and skill to his task.

Sunesis - putting pieces together like a puzzle; enables a person to intelligently assess a situation.

ENDNOTES

Chapter 1

1. Justin D. Long. "Beyond," phone call March 21, 2019.

2. James Strong, S.T.D., LL.D. "A Concise Dictionary of the Words in the Greek Testament; with Their Renderings in the Authorized English Version." In *Strong's Exhaustive Concordance of the Bible* (McLean, VA: MacDonald Publishing Company, n.d.), 26.

3. Alvin Toffler, *Power Shifts: Knowledge, Wealth, and Violence at the Edge of the 21st Century* (New York, NY: Bantam Books, 1990).

4. Robert L. Alden, Proverbs: *A Commentary on an Ancient Book of Timeless Advice* (Grand Rapids, MI: Baker Book House, 1983), 202. Alan Richardson, D.D. *A Theological Word Book of the Bible* (New York, NY: The MacMillan Company, 1950), 277. George Arthur Buttrick, ed.; The Interpreter's Bible: *The Holy Scriptures in the King James and Revised Standard Versions with General Articles and Introduction, Exegesis, Exposition for Each Book of the Bible, Vol. IV* (New York, NY: Abingdon Press, 1955), 944. *The Amplified Bible* (Grand Rapids, MI: Zondervan Bible Publishers, 1965), 740.

5. Frank E. Gaebelein (gen. ed.) and J.D. Douglas (assoc. ed.), *The Expositor's Bible Commentary with The New International Version of The Holy Bible, Volume 10, Romans–Galatians* (Grand Rapids, MI: Regency Reference Library, Zondervan Publishing House, 1976), 207–208.

6. James Strong, S.T.D., LL.D. "A Concise Dictionary of the Words in the Greek Testament," 70.

Chapter 2

1. Frank S. Mead, ed. and comp. *The Encyclopedia of Religious Quotations* (Old Tappan, NJ: Fleming H. Revell Co., 1976), 602.

2. William J. Lederer and Eugene Burdick, *The Ugly American* (New York, NY: W.W. Norton & Company, Inc., 1958), 145.

3. Ibid, 71.

4. Ibid, 71–72.

5. Roy & Revel Hession, *The Calvary Road* (Fort Washington, PA: Christian Literature Crusade, 1950, 1977), 89.

6. W. E. Vine, *Vine's Expository Dictionary of New Testament Words, Complete and Unabridged* (Westwood, NJ: Barbour and Company, Inc., 1940, 1952), 89.

7. Ibid, 272, 273, 347–348. James Strong, S.T.D., LL.D. "A Concise Dictionary of the Words in the Greek Testament...," 74. Gerhard Kittel & Gerhard Friedrich (translated by Geoffrey W. Bromiley), *Theological Dictionary of the New Testament* (Grand Rapids, MI: William B. Eerdmans Publishing Company, 1985) 152, 182, 1242.

8. Pius Wakatama, *Independence for the Third World Church: An African's Perspective on Missionary Work* (Downers Grove, IL: InterVarsity Press, 1976), 93–94.

9. William J. Lederer and Eugene Burdick, *The Ugly American* (New York, NY: W.W. Norton & Company, Inc., 1958), 277.

10. Wakatama, *Independence for the Third World Church: An African's Perspective on Missionary Work*, 14.

11. Chuck Bennett, "The Problem with Success," *Evangelical Missions Quarterly* 32, no. 1 (January, 1996): 20–26.

12. Wakatama, *Independence for the Third World Church: An African's Perspective on Missionary Work*, 89.

13. Lederer and Burdick, *The Ugly American*, 40.

14. Stephen E. Saint, "The Unfinished Mission to the 'Aucas,'" *Christianity Today* 42, no. 3 (March 2, 1998): 42–45.

15. Vinita Hampton and Carol Plueddemann, *World Shapers: A Treasury of Quotes from Great Missionaries* (Wheaton, IL: Harold Shaw Publishers, 1991), 59.

16. David Zac Niringiye, "Africans in missions: The possible dream," *Evangelical Missions Quarterly* 31, no. 1 (January 1995): 54-61.

Chapter 3

1. O. Henry, "The Gift of the Magi." In *The Complete Works of O. Henry*, vol. 1 (Garden City, NY: Doubleday & Company, Inc., 1899, 1953), 7-10.

2. Don Richardson, "The Hidden Message of Acts." In *Perspectives on the World Christian Movement: A Reader, Revised Edition*, ed. by Ralph D. Winter and Stephen C. Hawthorne (Pasadena, CA: William Carey Library, 1981, 1992), A110-A111.

3. Horace L. Fenton Jr., *Myths About Missions* (Downers Grove, IL: InterVarsity Press, 1973), 63.

4. Ruth A. Tucker, *From Jerusalem to Irian Jaya: A Biographical History of Christian Missions* (Grand Rapids, MI: Academie Books, Zondervan Publishing House, 1983), 67.

5. Jim Reapsome, "From the Catbird's Seat: The Truth About Unreached Peoples," *Evangelical Missions Quarterly* 30, no. 1 (January, 1994): 2-3.

6. Wakatama, *Independence for the Third World Church: An African's Perspective on Missionary Work*, 42.

7. John Stott, *One People: Helping Your Church Become a Caring Community* (Old Tappan, NJ: Fleming H. Revell Company, 1946, 1973), 30.

8. Ibid, 87.

9. Fenton, *Myths About Missions*, 69.

10. Ibid, p. 14.

Chapter 4

1. Tucker, *From Jerusalem to Irian Jaya: A Biographical History of Christian Missions*, 455-456.

2. Bruce Larson, *Living Out the Book of Acts* (Dallas, TX: Word Publishing, 1984), 22–23.

3. Ibid, 25–26.

4. Andrew Murray, *Waiting on God* (USA: Whitaker House, 1981, 1983), 11.

5. K.P. Yohannan, *Why the World Waits: Exposing the Reality of Modern Missions* (Lake Mary, FL: Creation House, 1991), 44.

Chapter 5

1. Hampton and Pleuderman, *World Shapers: A Treasury of Quotes from Great Missionaries*, 74.

2. Charles F. Pfeiffer and Everett F. Harrison, ed., *The Wycliffe Bible Commentary* (Chicago, IL: Moody Press, 1962), 212.

3. R. Laird Harris, ed; Gleason L. Archer Jr. and Bruce K. Waltke, assoc. ed., *Theological Wordbook of the Old Testament, vol. 1* (Chicago, IL: Moody Press, 1980), 620–621.

4. Pfeiffer and Harrison, ed., *The Wycliffe Bible Commentary*, 207.

5. Alfred Edersheim, Bible History: *Old Testament* (Peabody, MA: Hendrickson Publishers, Inc., 1995), 309.

6. Patrick Johnstone, *Operation World* (Grand Rapids, MI: Zondervan Publishing House, 1993), 336–338.

7. Edersheim, *Bible History: Old Testament*, 309.

8. Solomon Aryeetey, MD, Untitled article, *Evangelical Missions Quarterly* 31, no. 1 (January, 1995): 58.

9. Hampton and Pleuderman, *World Shapers: A Treasury of Quotes from Great Missionaries*, 31.

10. "Leading Article: Flocking to a Hotter Gospel." *The Daily Telegraph* (London), 16 October 1991, p. 20.

11. David Martin, "Catholic Church in Latin America Now Has Many Competitors," *The San Diego Union Tribune*, 7 April 1991, sec. C, p. 1.

12. This terminology comes from Edward R. Dayton and David A. Fraser, *Planning Strategies for World Evangelization, Revised Edition,* (Grand Rapids,

MI and Monrovia, CA: William B. Eerdmans Publishing Company and MARC, 1990).

13. Thomas H. McAlpine, *By Word, Work and Wonder: Cases in Holistic Mission* (Monrovia, CA: MARC, A Division of World Vision, 1995), 90.

Chapter 6

1. Merrill F. Unger, *Unger's Bible Dictionary* (Chicago, IL: Moody Press, 1957, 1985), 67.

2. Ibid, 631, 881–886, 890–893.

3. James Strong, S.T.D., LL.D. "A Concise Dictionary of the Words in the Hebrew Bible; With Their Renderings in the Authorized English Version." In *Strong's Exhaustive Concordance of the Bible*, 73. W. E. Vine, *Vine's Expository Dictionary of New Testament Words, Complete and Unabridged*, 58–59.

4. Hampton and Pleuderman, *World Shapers: A Treasury of Quotes from Great Missionaries*, 100.

5. F. Kefa Sempangi, with Barbara R. Thompson, *A Distant Grief: The Real Story Behind the Martyrdom of Christians in Uganda* (Glendale, CA: Regal Books, A Division of G/L Publications, 1979), 90–91.

6. Marguerite G. Kraft, *Understanding Spiritual Power: A Forgotten Dimension of Cross-Cultural Mission and Ministry* (Maryknoll, NY: Orbis Books, 1995), 14–19.

7. "Layman's Testimony Touches Eight Villages with Gospel," <WebServant@imb.org>, *Southern Baptist Convention International Mission Board: News Stories*, (accessed April 21, 1998).

8. K.P. Yohannan, *Why the World Waits: Exposing the Reality of Modern Missions*, 170, 174.

9. Alan R. Tippett, *People Movements in Southern Polynesia: Studies in the Dynamics of Church-planting and Growth in Tahiti, New Zealand, Tonga, and Samoa* (Chicago, IL: Moody Press, 1971), 16.

10. Ken Baker, "Power Encounter and Church Planting," *Evangelical Missions Quarterly* 26, no. 3 (July 1990): 306–312.

11. F. Kefa Sempangi, *A Distant Grief*, 83–87.

12. Ibid.

13. Charles Kraft, "What Kind of Encounters Do We Need in Our Christian Witness?" *Evangelical Missions Quarterly* 27, no. 3 (July, 1991), 258–265.

Chapter 7

1. David F. Wells. "Prayer: Rebelling Against the Status Quo." *Perspectives on the World Christian Movement: A Reader, Revised Edition*, ed. Winter & Hawthorne, (Pasadena, CA: William Carey Library, 1981, 1992), A144–A147.

APPENDICES

Appendix 1:

AIMS has a new President! On January 1, 2019, Joshua Bold was inaugurated by the AIMS board as President. I am now Founder/ President Emeritus. It is my honor to serve Joshua and the AIMS team in this role.

Joshua Bold is husband to Bevin, father to Haven and Honor, minister, and missionary mobilizer. He attended Bible college in 2005 after being supernaturally delivered from drug addiction. While Joshua struggled with addiction, Bevin did missionary work in Uzbekistan and Mexico.

He and Bevin are committed to reaching the unreached people groups of the earth. Their desire to serve the nations stemmed from heartfelt prayers saying, "Break our hearts for what breaks Yours." In 2008, they moved to Iraq to serve the Kurdish people for five years. They planted a house church, baptized former Muslims, and opened a café.

In 2013, God expanded their ministry into Europe, the Middle East, and North Africa. They served as missions pastors in New Mexico for six years, while serving as the Middle East/North Africa coordinators for AIMS.

Appendix 2:

Do you want to change the world? Join with AIMS in its initiative to adopt and begin church planting movements in 3,500 unreached people groups (UPGs). Every individual, church, organization, and business can be involved.

AIMS can guide you in selecting and adopting a UPG, then will provide coaching and training in the ongoing process. AIMS will connect you with a trained indigenous missionary who will give you reports of the progress. Your coach can expand this partnership by connecting you with other individuals, churches, organizations, and businesses that have made an adoption commitment. These partnerships are how AIMS has seen an average of six churches planted every day for the past 24 years. Help AIMS increase this to 50–100 per day!

Let's partner together in changing the world! Contact AIMS at 719-266-3737 or email aims@aims.org.

Appendix 3:

You have a desire to share the gospel, but if you and your church don't have scriptural vision and practical application, little will happen. In *Harvest Connection*, Dr. Howard Foltz shares thought-provoking insights gleaned from more than fifty years in missions leadership. You will learn how to motivate and equip yourself and your church to take part in God's great final harvest.

Harvest Connection dives into the following mission essentials:

- **Foundation.** The Great Commission defined for today
- **Motivation.** The urgency that must be felt by genuine believers
- **Leadership.** How to spread the vision to your church

- **Targeting.** Why local and overseas ministries must be targeted to be effective
- **Sending.** The nuts and bolts of successful missionary sending
- **Financing.** Sufficient financing that does not serve as a distraction
- **Prayer.** The only way to begin and support a ministry initiative

ABOUT THE AUTHOR

DR. HOWARD FOLTZ, and his wife Pat have been missionaries since 1963. He began his ministry by pioneering the Dallas/Fort Worth Teen Challenge programs. Then this pioneering vision, under Dr. Foltz' leadership, expanded the Teen Challenge ministry into 27 countries. Hundreds, even thousands, of drug addicts and people with life controlling problems have been saved, and many are now pastors and missionaries.

In 1985, Dr. Foltz founded *Acceleration In Mission Strategies* (AIMS), a missions program based on the principles of this book, to focus on finishing the Great Commission seen in Acts 1:8. The focus of AIMS is to target and reach unreached people groups. Tens of thousands of pastors and leaders have been trained by AIMS and thousands of churches planted by these indigenous partners among unreached people groups. Dr. Foltz speaks not only from his experience in Teen Challenge but also from his 24 years serving as professor of Global Evangelism at Regent University. He has written three other books, traveled to over 100 countries, and is a highly respected national and international missions teacher.